CAVENDISH PRACT

Executorship and Administration of Estates

SECOND EDITION

ROLAND D'COSTA
DISTRICT PROBATE REGISTRAR, OXFORD

SERIES EDITOR
CM BRAND, SOLICITOR

Cavendish Publishing Limited

London • Sydney

Second edition first published in Great Britain 2001 by Cavendish Publishing Limited, The Glass House, Wharton Street, London WC1X 9PX, United Kingdom
Telephone: +44 (0)20 7278 8000   Facsimile: +44 (0)20 7278 8080
Email: info@cavendishpublishing.com
Website: www.cavendishpublishing.com

©   D'Costa, R   2001

All rights reserved. No part of this publication may be reproduced, stored in a retrieval system, or transmitted, in any form or by any means, electronic, mechanical, photocopying, recording, scanning or otherwise, except under the terms of the Copyright Designs and Patents Act 1988 or under the terms of a licence issued by the Copyright Licensing Agency, 90 Tottenham Court Road, London W1P 9HE, UK, without the permission in writing of the publisher.

British Library Cataloguing in Publication Data

D'Costa, R R (Roland R)
Executorship and administration of estates – 2nd ed – (Practice notes series)
1 Executors and administrators – England 2 Executors and administrators – Wales 3 Decedants' estates – England 4 Decedants' estates – Wales
I Title
346.4'2'056

ISBN 1 85941 459 1

Printed and bound in Great Britain

Contents

Glossary ix

1 Basic Information 1
    1.1 Introduction 1
    1.2 Sources 1
    1.3 Grants of representation 2
    1.4 Choice of personal representative 2
    1.5 Renunciations 5

2 First Steps: Pre-Grant Preparation 7
    2.1 First steps 7
    2.2 Instruction checklist 7
    2.3 Action upon receiving instructions 9
    2.4 The role of personal representatives 10
    2.5 Ascertaining the estate for the grant 11
    2.6 Necessity for a grant 12
    2.7 Exceptions 13
    2.8 Payment of death duties and court fees 14

3 Application for a Grant of Representation 15
    3.1 Contentious and non-contentious business distinguished 15
    3.2 Distribution of probate business in the High Court 16

3.3	Where to apply for a grant	16
3.4	Papers required	16
3.5	The probate computer system	17
3.6	The oath	19
3.7	Executor's oath	20
3.8	Oath for administration with will annexed	22
3.9	Administrator's oath	26
3.10	Foreign domicile	33
3.11	Non-Contentious Probate fees	42
3.12	Checklist for oaths	44
3.13	Papers to be lodged in a grant application	46

4 The Inland Revenue Account — 47

4.1	The Inland Revenue account	47
4.2	Excepted estates	47
4.3	Forms of account (deaths on or after 18 March 1986)	49
4.4	Delivery and payment of Inheritance Tax	50
4.5	Threshold for and rate of Inheritance Tax (1989 onwards)	51

5 Disputes and Impediments to the Making of a Grant — 53

5.1	Caveats (r 44)	53
5.2	Central index of pending applications and caveats	54
5.3	Reasons for entering a caveat	54
5.4	Sequence of steps following the entry of a caveat	55
5.5	Warning and appearance	56

5.6	Probate claims	56
5.7	Citations	57
5.8	Issuing a summons	58
5.9	Standing search	59

6 Administration of the estate 61

6.1	Priority for debts and liabilities	61
6.2	The practitioner's role	61
6.3	Payments of debts, etc	62
6.4	Registration and distribution	63
6.5	Variations and disclaimers	64
6.6	Trust arrangements	65
6.7	Estate accounts and practitioner's costs	66

7 Forms 69

7.1	Affidavit of due execution	69
7.2	Affidavit of handwriting	70
7.3	Affidavit of plight and condition	71
7.4	Affidavit of search for a will	72
7.5	Affidavit in support of a privileged will	73
7.6	Affidavit of identity	73
7.7	Affidavit in support of application for order to be appointed to obtain administration on behalf of a minor (r 32(2))	74
7.8	Renunciation of probate (r 37)	75
7.9	Renunciation of administration with will (r 37)	76
7.10	Renunciation of administration (r 37)	77

7.11	Renunciation of probate by two partners of a firm (r 37(2)(a))	77
7.12	Retraction of renunciation (r 37(3))	78
7.13	Caveat	79
7.14	Warning to caveator (r 44(5))	80
7.15	Appearance to warning or citation (rr 44(10), 47(4) and 48(2)(b))	81
7.16	Standing search (r 43)	81
7.17	Summons	82
7.18	Nomination of second administrator (r 32(3))	83
7.19	Account	84
7.20	Bill of costs	85
7.21	Section 27 notice	86
7.22	Advertisement for inclusion in a s 27 notice in the *London Gazette*	87
7.23	Deed of assignment/variation and disclaimer	87
7.24	Assent of freehold property	88
7.25	Receipt for legacies	89
7.26	Receipt for a bequest	89
7.27	Inland Revenue Account	90

8 Answers to Common Problems — 117

8.1	Matters that question due execution of a will	117
8.2	What evidence is required if the will contains alterations, obliterations or interlineations which have not been formally authenticated by the testator and the witnesses or the will is not dated?	119

8.3	The original will has tears or burn marks, has pin holes or paperclip indentations	119
8.4	The original will cannot be found; the applicant wishes to prove it as contained in a copy or a reconstruction	120
8.5	A sole executor who takes no benefit cannot be traced	120
8.6	Setting up a privileged will	121
8.7	The appointment of executor is ambiguous or appears to be void	121
8.8	The person entitled in priority to a grant of representation is mentally incapable	122
8.9	Remuneration to a professional executor	122

9 Useful Addresses 123

10 Further Reading 129

Glossary

accretion – increase in the value (of the estate)

***ad colligenda bona*, letters of administration** – a grant of representation to a fit person limited only to the collection and preservation of the estate of a deceased person and to specific acts ordered by the court where there is a danger of waste or loss of the estate and matters cannot wait for a representative to be appointed in the normal way

administration, letters of – a grant of representation made when a deceased person dies intestate

administration with will annexed, letters of – a grant of representation made to a person who is not an executor of the will

administrator – a person appointed by the court to pay the debts and liabilities of the deceased and to distribute the estate according to law

appearance – a form which a person files in court in acknowledgment of certain documents sealed by the court which he has received

assent – transfer of ownership; in the case of land, by a deed in writing

assignment – a deed in writing by which a person agrees to transfer all his prospective interest in an estate to another person

bequest – a gift made in a will

bona vacantia – property of a deceased person to which no one is entitled under the law

caveat – a notice filed in court by a person which prevents a grant of representation being sealed or issued without prior notice to himself

cessate, grant – a further grant of representation which is made after the reason or purpose for which a previous grant was made ceases to exist

chattels, personal – generally, all movable personal possessions of a person – more fully listed in s 55(1)(x) of the Administration of Estates Act 1925

citation – a notice under the seal of the court which requires an executor named in a will to obtain or refuse probate or a person who is entitled to any part of deceased's estate to obtain or refuse letters of administration (including any will) or a person who has an interest under a will to prove the validity of a will in solemn form

codicil – a testamentary document which amends, extends or explains a will

contrary interest – an interest of another person which prejudices a person's right to grant or to his beneficial entitlement to an estate

de bonis non (administratis), **letters of administration** – a further grant of representation which is made because the administrator of the previous grant died leaving estate unadministered or without having completed its administration

devise; devisee – a gift of real property given by a will; the person to whom the gift is given

domicile – a place, usually a State with its own system of law, in which a person has his permanent residence or in which he has made an intention to reside permanently after first establishing a physical presence

double probate, grant of – a further grant of the whole estate of a deceased person to an executor who was not named in a previous grant

excepted estate – property of a deceased person which falls within certain values and conditions for which an Inland Revenue account does not have to be prepared before a grant may issue

executor – a person whom the deceased person has appointed by his will to administer his will and estate

executor de son tort – a person who has intermeddled in the estate of a deceased person without authority of the court

ex parte **(without notice)** – an application to the court, usually for an order for which a summons or written notice is not required to be served on any other person

fiat copy – a reproduction, either by facsimile or engrossment, of a testamentary paper omitting unattested alterations or additions it contains and, where appropriate, restoring unattested deletions and which copy or engrossment the court has directed to be proved

grant of representation – probate or letters of administration (including one with will annexed) under seal of the court

guardian – a person (other than a child's father or mother) whom the court appoints or who may qualify under a statute to have parental responsibility for a minor child (see parental responsibility)

heir – (in foreign domicile cases) a person entitled by law to inherit or succeed to property

intermeddle – deal with the deceased's property without first obtaining a grant to his estate

intestate – a person who dies without having made a will

legacy; legatee – a gift of personal property; the recipient of such a gift

minority interest – the interest of a person who has not attained 18 years of age in the estate of a deceased person

non-contentious probate – obtaining of a grant of probate or administration where there is no dispute by way of a probate claim of a person's entitlement to the grant

nuncupative will – a will which does not exist in written form; an oral will

oath – a sworn document in which an applicant for a grant recites the details applicable to the deceased and his estate, his title to the grant and his promise to perform his duties as an administrator of the estate

parental responsibility – all rights, duties and responsibilities in respect of a minor (child) which are held by a person or local authority who is entitled to exercise them under the Children Act 1989

personal estate – property which does not include immovables or real property (see chattels)

personal representative – an executor who proves his testator's will; an administrator of the deceased's estate appointed by the court

probate, grant of – a document under seal issued by the court granting administration of an estate to an executor named in a will

propound – prove a will or testamentary document in solemn form

real estate – land including buildings on it and natural assets such as timber and minerals; leasehold of land or buildings

renunciation – a document by which a person entitled to a grant of representation gives up that right

retraction – a document by which a person who has renounced representation of an estate withdraws his renunciation after he has been given permission to do so by the court

testator – a person who has made a will

trust corporation – an individual who by his official position, or a corporation which is empowered by law (Public Trustee Act 1906 and Trustee Act 1925) to undertake trust business

vest in – transfer (of ownership) to

void for uncertainty, appointment of executor – appointment of executor not capable of taking effect because the testator's intention as written in the will is not clear or cannot be put into practice

warning – a notice to a person who has entered a caveat requiring him to show his interest an take appropriate action as prescribed in the Non-Contentious Probate Rules 1987

1 Basic Information

1.1 Introduction

This work explains the need for a grant of representation to a deceased person's estate, the requirement for an application for a grant and the duties of a personal representative. It describes the role of a solicitor or probate practitioner in extracting a grant of representation. Reference is made to other texts from time to time, but this is kept to a minimum.

1.2 Sources

The law and practice affecting estates of deceased persons and the duties of personal representatives is regulated by statute, case law, statutory instruments and practice directions.

Common statutes are:
- Wills Act 1837;
- Administration of Estates Act 1925;
- Law of Property Act 1925;
- Trustee Act 1925;
- Settled Land Act 1925;
- Wills Act 1963;
- Supreme Court Act 1981;
- Administration of Justice Act 1982;
- Inheritance Tax Act 1984.

The Non-Contentious Probate Rules 1987 SI 1987/2024 (as amended 1991, 1998 and 1999) govern the practice and procedure for applications for grants of representation. In this work, reference to these Probate Rules is denoted by the prefix 'r'. Other statutory instruments are the

Non-Contentious Probate Fees Order 1999 SI 1999/688 (as amended 2000) (see 3.11) and the Inheritance Tax (Delivery of Accounts) Regulations 2000 SI 2000/967.

1.3 Grants of representation

There are three types of grants of representation:
- probate;
- letters of administration (with will annexed); and
- letters of administration.

Grants may be obtained either by application to the Principal Registry of the Family Division (the Principal Registry) or to any district probate registry or sub-registry (r 4, and see Chapters 3 and 9).

Apart from an application by a personal applicant (r 5), an application may be submitted either by a solicitor (r 4) or a probate practitioner (rr 2(1) and 4). At the present time, probate practitioners are barristers and notaries public. For ease of reference, I have used the term 'practitioner' to describe either a solicitor or probate practitioner in this work. Probate rules require a practitioner to give the address of his place of business in England and Wales (r 4). Occasionally, a registrar may require a practitioner to confirm his right to practise by producing a copy of his practising certificate.

Note: ss 54 and 55 of the Courts and Legal Services Act 1990, which remove the restriction imposed by s 23 of the Solicitors Act 1974 on persons who may prepare probate papers, have not been fully implemented. When this happens, classes of practitioner will be extended to include banks, building societies, insurance companies, trustee and executor companies and members of bodies as approved by the Lord Chancellor.

1.4 Choice of personal representative

1.4.1 Executor

A person who makes a will is called a testator, and an executor is someone appointed by him to execute his will on his death. This appointment is made in the body of the will. A bare appointment of an executor in a document which does not specify any duties for him, nor makes any legacy or devise, may not be sufficient to make it a will. An exception would be a codicil, which revokes a previous appointment of executor and substitutes a new one.

Where a testator does not expressly appoint an executor, but he directs a person to perform duties such as paying debts and distributing gifts out of the general estate, this would imply an appointment, and the court would usually construe that person as executor according to the tenor of the will. A plain appointment of a trustee will not be treated as executor according to tenor.

An executor is a person whom the testator trusts and relies upon to administer his estate. He derives his title from the will and the property of his testator vests in him from the moment of the testator's death. The executor may refuse the appointment by renouncing it, but he cannot assign it to another person (see 1.5). An executor provides evidence of his title by applying to the court to prove the will and obtaining a grant of probate (see 3.7). Thus, the grant of probate is proof of the executor's title.

1.4.2 Earliest time for a grant of probate

The probate registry will not issue a grant of probate within seven days of a testator's death except with leave of a district judge or registrar (r 6(2)).

1.4.3 Chain of representation

An executor who proves his testator's will becomes also the executor of any will of which probate was granted to the testator who, at the date of his own death, was the sole or last surviving executor named in the grant. This process is called a chain of representation. The chain passes on or transmits to an executor any offices of executor as described above (s 7 of the Administration of Estates Act 1925). The chain may move upwards or downwards without limit. The main requirement is that the will of the sole or last surviving executor is proved by his executor.

The chain is broken by:
- intestacy;
- failure of a testator to appoint an executor; or
- failure to obtain probate of a will.

1.4.4 Administrator

An administrator is appointed by the court in accordance with Probate Rules if a testator failed to appoint an executor, if the appointment of executor fails (3.8) or if the deceased died intestate (3.9). The order of priority for appointing an administrator is dictated by r 20 (3.8.1) where the deceased made a will, or r 22 (3.9.1) where he died intestate or partially intestate. The rules take into account the beneficial interest of various classes or persons. Special rules apply if the person who would otherwise be entitled to apply for a grant is a minor (3.9.3) or is mentally incapable (8.8). Such a person may not extract a grant in his own right, and administrators are selected to obtain administration for his use and benefit in accordance with r 32 or r 35.

The order or priority may be bypassed if the person entitled to obtain a grant is not available, or is unable to take a grant, or some other person seeks to override his interest. In such cases, application may be made to the court to exercise its discretion and order that some other person may have leave to obtain administration of the estate (s 116 of the Supreme Court Act 1981).

An administrator's authority over an estate commences from the moment the grant of administration is issued.

1.4.5 Title prior to grant of administration

The real and personal estate of a person who dies wholly intestate vests in the Public Trustee until a grant of administration is obtained (s 14 of the Law of Property (Miscellaneous Provisions) Act 1994, amending s 9 of the Administration of Estates Act 1925). Similarly, if a will does not dispose of all the estate and no executor is appointed, or there is no executor with power to obtain probate, the real and personal estate of the deceased vests in the Public Trustee until a grant of representation is obtained. A landlord who wishes to terminate a tenancy of a tenant who dies intestate should serve a notice to quit on the Public Trustee by sending it to the Public Trustee, Stewart House, 24 Kingsway, London WC2B 6JX.

1.4.6 Earliest time for a grant of administration

Except with leave of the court, the probate registry will not issue:
- a grant of administration (with will annexed) within seven days of the deceased's death; or

- a grant of administration within 14 days of the deceased's death (r 6(2)).

1.5 Renunciations

A person entitled to a grant of representation may decline the office by filing a renunciation. It should be absolute and unconditional, in writing and witnessed by a disinterested person. It becomes final upon being filed in the probate registry (*Re Morant's Goods* (1874) LR 3 P&D 151). The renunciation of an executor who has intermeddled will not be accepted and it will be declared invalid (*Re Bigg's Estate* [1966] P 118).

A renunciation may only by retracted by leave of the court (r 37(3)). (See Chapter 7 for precedents for forms of renunciation and retraction.)

2 First Steps: Pre-Grant Preparation

2.1 First steps

Upon receiving instructions to obtain a grant of representation to a deceased person's estate, the practitioner should make an assessment of the client's prior entitlement to a grant either in his own right or jointly with others (see Chapter 3). This will, of course, vary depending upon whether the deceased left a will or died intestate. The practitioner will call for and examine any original wills (including codicils) which the deceased made. If an original will cannot be found, but there are grounds to believe that one may be in existence, make a search. Besides searching the deceased's possessions and places where he kept personal documents, reasonable steps would include inquiries of solicitors, accountants or banks which the deceased was known to deal with. The Probate Department at the Principal Registry or a probate registry may be requested to search for any will deposited for safe custody by the deceased during his lifetime (s 126 of the Supreme Court Act 1981, and, when implemented, ss 23–26 of the Administration of Justice Act 1982). A probate registry will search the probate computer database to provide details of any will deposited, but the request to release the will must be made to the Probate Department. Where a will which a deceased made cannot be found and it remains unrevoked, or was known to be in existence after the death of the testator, an application to prove a copy or a reconstruction of the will is necessary (see 7.3).

2.2 Instruction checklist

Details of the deceased are a prerequisite to preparation of papers for a grant. The reference will include the following:

Clients

- names, addresses, telephone numbers;
- title to grant of representation and relationship to the deceased.

Deceased

- names (including alias names) and last address;
- testate/intestate;
- location of any testamentary papers/memorandum of wishes;
- domicile;
- dates of birth and death – obtain death certificate;
- personal status – married, bachelor, spinster, divorced (single), widowed – obtain marriage certificate and original or certified copy of decree absolute of divorce/nullity;
- next of kin (including dependants);
- funeral arrangements - burial/cremation.

Assets

- stocks and shares;
- bank accounts;
- National Savings Bank, building and friendly or co-operative society accounts;
- premium bonds and National Savings certificates;
- unit trusts, bonds and other investment accounts (PEPs, Tessas, etc);
- insurance policies;
- cash in hand;
- jewellery and antiques;
- other chattels;
- rents;
- arrears of salary/pension;
- real estate (including leaseholds) – location and title deeds.

Debts

- mortgage;
- gas, electricity, telephone;

- water rates, council tax;
- credit cards;
- loans;
- other.

Other details

- accountant;
- stockbroker;
- solicitor;
- tax district and reference/National Insurance number;
- property insurance – home, contents, car, etc;
- gifts made within the last seven years of death:

    (a) description and date;

    (b) donee (name and address);

    (c) amount or value of gift;
- beneficiaries – names and addresses.

This list is not exhaustive. A record should be made of any relevant information.

2.3 Action upon receiving instructions

The point at which a practitioner becomes involved in the affairs of the deceased is crucial to the role he plays in securing and preserving the estate. For example, if he receives instructions soon after death, his actions could include:

- registration of death with the Registrar of Births and Deaths for the area in which death occurred;
- obtaining sufficient copies of the death certificate to send for registration to institutions who hold the assets of the deceased. Institutions such as banks and insurance companies require an official copy death certificate before noting the death in their records. Some of these institutions may be prepared to release small assets upon production of the death certificate without requiring a grant of representation (see 2.7);
- arrangements for the funeral if these have not already been made. It is important that the deceased's wishes for this, whether contained in his will or a memorandum of wishes, are made known to the

executors or next of kin. A known executor has primary responsibility for the funeral and he is entitled to obtain possession of it (*Sharp v Lush* (1879) 10 Ch D 468; *Dobson v North Tyneside Health Authority* [1997] 1 WLR 596). The executor derives his authority from the will. Otherwise this responsibility falls on the next of kin. The deceased may be entitled to a funeral allowance under the Social Fund Maternity and Funeral Expenses General Regulations 1987 SI 1987/481, but the DSS may recover this from the estate (s 32(4) of the Social Security Act 1986). A means tested recipient may claim a funeral payment in respect of a deceased person from the Social Fund if he takes responsibility for the funeral;

- safeguard and secure empty and rented property. If the deceased's dwelling is unoccupied, valuables such as money, share certificates, insurance policies, bonds and other certificates of value, jewellery and other valuables should be removed for safekeeping;
- arrangements for removal and housing of pets;
- arrangements for gas, electricity and water services to be turned off at the mains or terminated by the companies concerned;
- stopping deliveries of milk, newspapers, etc;
- informing managing agents of any of the deceased's property let to tenants. Otherwise, arranging for the rents to be paid to a nominated account;
- checking insurance of property, contents and motor vehicles. Any that do not meet current market values to be increased (but see s 19 of the Trustee Act 1925);
- informing employers/pension administrators/social security office as appropriate of the death;
- informing banks and building societies. These will usually require to see the death certificate. Large current account balances to be transferred to (higher deposit) deposit accounts.

2.4 The role of personal representatives

2.4.1 Executors and administrators distinguished

The term 'personal representative' covers executors and administrators (s 55(1)(xi) of the Administration of Estates Act 1925). It includes with regard to liability for death duties any person who intermeddles in the estate of the deceased without authority (executor *de son tort*).

An executor derives his title from his testator's will. The grant of probate provides the evidence of that title. A grant of administration appoints an administrator. A grant of administration with will annexed is proof of that will. Such a grant prevents any executor named in the will from acting in the administration of the estate.

After a grant of administration is made, the administrator has the same powers as if he were an executor, except that he is not included in any chain of representation (see 1.4.3).

2.4.2 Duties of personal representatives

The grant thus constitutes proof of the appointment of a personal representative. Section 25 of the Administration of Estates Act 1925, as amended by s 9 of the Administration of Estates Act 1971, prescribes the duty of a personal representative to:

- collect and get in the real and personal estate of the deceased and administer it according to law;
- when required to do so by the court, exhibit on oath in the court a full inventory of the estate and when required, render an account of the administration of the estate to the court; and
- when required to do so by the High Court, deliver up the grant of probate or administration to that court.

2.5 Ascertaining the estate for the grant

The assets revealed from inquiries flowing from the checklist detailed in 2.2 should be itemised and valued as at the date of death. These will include written valuations or quotations of:

- real estate (including leaseholds) by estate agents or valuers, unless the estate is small and it is evident that the net value of it is within the Inheritance Tax threshold;
- property held jointly with other persons. The deceased's interest ceases on his death if he held the property with another person as a joint tenant beneficially (s 3(4) of the Administration of Estates Act 1925). On the other hand, if a deceased did have a beneficial interest in a tenancy in common, his share of the property vests in the personal representative;
- the deceased's business (his will may contain special powers concerning business assets and goodwill);

- shares – given by a stockbroker or, in the case of unquoted shares, by the company secretary. If the value of the shares is small, the practitioner may find it convenient to quote the value from the *Financial Times* at the date of death;
- jewellery, pictures, antiques, stamp and coin collections, cars, etc;
- arrears of income or pension due to the deceased and any benefits due to the estate arising out of the death, for example, a lump sum payment;
- balance of bank and building society accounts;
- premium bonds, national saving certificates;
- insurance policies on the deceased's life, unit trusts, etc;
- rents;
- benefits payable under social security laws (note: (a) the deceased's entitlement to benefits such as invalidity, sickness and income support and unemployment cease after the week in which death occurred; (b) benefits which were recoverable from the deceased during his lifetime may be claimed either from the estate or personally from the personal representatives (*Secretary of State for Social Services v Solly* [1974] 3 All ER 922));
- the deceased's interest in any unadministered estate.

The debts and liabilities will include:
- the funeral account (this may include a reasonable amount for mourning and a tombstone or headstone marking the deceased's grave);
- loans and overdraft;
- credit card payments;
- nursing and other medical services;
- council tax, water rates, electricity, gas, telephone, etc;
- mortgages.

2.6 Necessity for a grant

2.6.1 Executor

An executor takes his title from the will, and this appointment begins at the moment of the testator's death.

The executor may seize and take possession of his testator's goods, pay, release and receive debts. He may sell any of the testator's estate which he holds on trust for sale or which has not been disposed by the will. However, a purchaser may withhold payment until he has seen the grant of probate (*Re Stevens* [1897] 1 Ch 422). Section 36 of the Administration of Estates Act 1925 requires an indorsement of assent to be made on the grant where a purchase of land is involved. An executor may be sued before probate, and he too may begin a claim in his representative capacity, but he will be required to produce the grant for inspection by the defendant in evidence at the trial (*Webb v Adkins* (1854) 14 CB 401), or before the final order is perfected.

Probate is required to deal in real property and recover and receive personal property in the UK.

2.6.2 Administrator

Since an administrator's title derives from the grant, he may do nothing in that capacity until he obtains a grant of administration. An action or claim begun by him before the grant cannot be validated upon it being issued afterwards (*Ingall and Moran* [1944] KB 160; *Hilton v Sutton Steam Laundry* [1946] KB 65).

2.6.3 Jurisdiction of grant

Formerly, a grant was a sufficient title to all the deceased's property in England and Wales if he died domiciled in England and Wales. Sections 1–3 of the Administration of Estates Act 1971 extend this jurisdiction to the rest of the UK.

2.7 Exceptions

The Administration of Estates (Small Payments) Act 1965 schedules assets of a deceased person which may be paid out to a person entitled without the need for a grant. This Act and subsequent statutory instruments (Administration of Estates (Small Payments) (Increase of Limit) Orders 1975 and 1984) vary the amount payable according to the date of death:

Payment	Deaths on or after
£500	5 September 1965
£1,500	10 August 1975
£5,000	11 May 1984

- assets covered – monies in:
  - (i) a particular fund which are due to the deceased because of his employment or special situation during his lifetime (includes pay and pension);
  - (ii) a particular fund unrelated to employment – these include government stock, government or savings bank annuities, accounts with registered societies, national insurance and funds in court;
- nominations made by the deceased under pension and insurance schemes do not usually require the production of a grant;
- a *donatio mortis causa* – a gift which a person suffering from a serious illness makes in the belief that death is imminent. The main requirement is that the gift is made in contemplation of and conditional only on the death of the donor and that there is actual or constructive delivery of the gift. A grant is not required to deal with such a gift;
- some institutions may be prepared to release small assets without the need for a grant.

2.8 Payment of death duties and court fees

The assets or income of the estate are frozen from the date of death and cannot be used to pay Inheritance Tax and court fees. If there is insufficient cash in hand to meet these payments, it is advisable to open a bank account in the name of the personal representative so that money may be borrowed to discharge these liabilities.

Sometimes, banks or building societies with whom the deceased kept their account may agree to account directly to the court for fees or to the Inland Revenue for Inheritance Tax by issuing a bankers draft or crossed cheques. Similar arrangements may be made if the deceased held money with National Savings, saving certificates or premium bonds.

3 Application for a Grant of Representation

3.1 Contentious and non-contentious business distinguished

Section 25 of the Supreme Court Act 1981 confers on the High Court the jurisdiction in relation to:
- testamentary causes or matters;
- the grant, amendment or revocation of probate and letters of administration; and
- the real and personal estate of deceased persons.

Contentious business is the issue and disposal of probate proceedings where a dispute has arisen over the validity of the will of a deceased person or concerning the obtaining or revocation of a grant. The dispute is one which usually cannot be resolved by application under the Probate Rules.

A probate claim which starts the proceedings may be for the grant or revocation of probate or letters of administration, or for an order pronouncing for or against an alleged will (Practice Direction supplementing Civil Procedure Rules 1998, Pt 49). A probate claim is begun in the Chancery Division of the High Court. A claim may be brought in a county court if the net value of the estate does not exceed the county court limit (currently £30,000) (s 32 of the County Courts Act 1984).

After the Chancery Division or county court makes an order granting probate or administration to some person or pronouncing for or against the validity of a will, the grant itself is issued out of the Family Division, the order being the basis of title which is referred to in the oath and the grant (r 7(1)(a); s 128 of the Supreme Court Act 1981: see below).

Non-contentious or common form probate business is defined by s 128 of the Supreme Court Act 1981 as the obtaining of probate or administration and administration where there is no contention (pending probate proceedings) as to the right to a grant. It includes:
- the passing of probates and administration through the High Court in contentious cases where the contest has been terminated;
- all business of a non-contentious nature in matters of testacy and intestacy not being proceedings in any action; and
- the business of lodging caveats against a grant of probate and administration (see Chapter 5).

3.2 Distribution of probate business in the High Court

Schedule 1 to the Supreme Court Act 1981 distributes to:
- the Chancery Division all causes and matters relating to the estates of deceased persons and probate business other than non-contentious or common form business; and
- the Family Division all causes and matters relating to non-contentious or common form business.

3.3 Where to apply for a grant

A practitioner may lodge an application for a grant at any one of the district probate registries or probate sub-registries or at the Probate Department in the Principal Registry of the Family Division (see Chapter 9 for addresses). The form of application is an oath prescribed by r 8. A sub-registry will process an application for a grant and deal with all correspondence. It will refer for directions any matters of difficulty to the registrar at its parent registry. The grant itself will issue from the parent registry.

3.4 Papers required

The practitioner lodges the following documents appropriate to the estate of the deceased:
- the oath;
- the will and any codicils and papers incorporated by reference;

- affidavit evidence to suit the circumstances of the case, for example, evidence of execution, plight and condition, handwriting, etc (practitioners may seek the registrar's directions for his requirement for such evidence prior to preparing the papers);
- if appropriate, Inland Revenue Form D18, controlled and receipted by the Capital Taxes Office (CTO) where Inheritance Tax is payable (see Chapter 4);
- probate fee (see 3.11).

3.5 The probate computer system

All applications for grants, caveats (Chapter 5), standing searches (Chapter 5), wills deposited for safe custody or on renunciation, contentious probate proceedings (which the Senior District Judge has been notified of by the Chancery Division or a county court) and grants of representation are recorded in the probate computer system (probateman). On receipt of an application, the probate registry enters its details and probateman automatically searches for any matching records. It is important that the details given in the oath are accurate. The name and dates of birth and death of the deceased given in the entry of the register of death should be included in the oath, as should any alias names by which the deceased was known or in which he held assets (District Judges' Direction, 12 January 1999). If the computer search discloses a matching entry which confirms an existing grant in respect of the same estate, another pending application, a caveat or probate proceedings, the probate registry will inform the practitioner of this result. Probateman is unable to distinguish between similar sounding names such as 'John Smith' and 'Jon Smyth'. It is, therefore, important that the practitioner discloses in the oath any variation of name by which the deceased was known. If an alias name for the deceased is required in the grant, the oath must specify at least one asset held in that name.

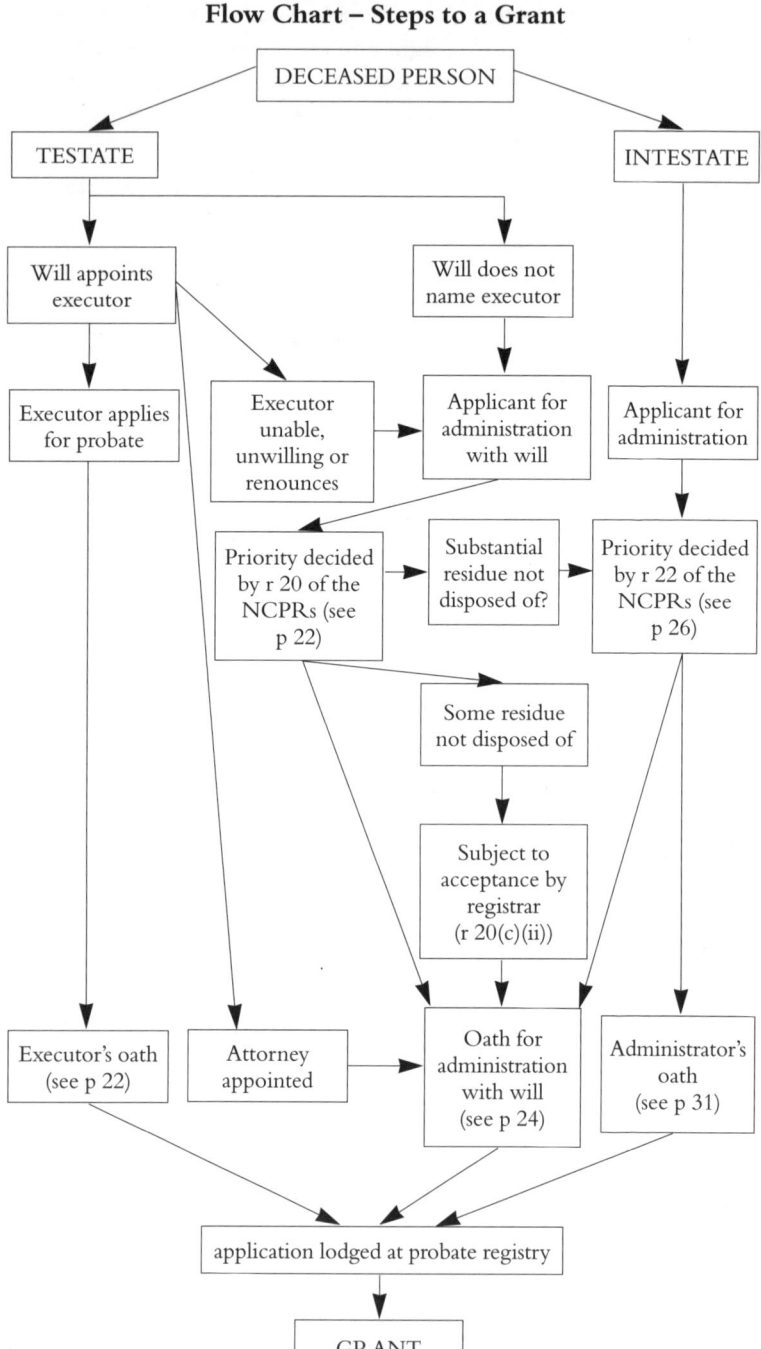

3.6 The oath

Every application for a grant or representation is made by an oath (r 8). The maximum number of applicants is four (s 114(1) of the Supreme Court Act 1981). At least two applicants or a trust corporation (with or without an individual) are required in any application for a grant of administration (including one with will annexed) if any beneficiary is a minor or if a life interest arises (s 114(2) of the Supreme Court Act 1981).

The applicant confirms:
- his identity and that of the deceased;
- the dates of birth and death of the deceased;
- the nature of any testamentary papers;
- the domicile of the deceased at the date of date (r 8(2));
- whether any land settled before the death of the deceased remains settled (r 8(3));
- whether life or minority interests arise (r 8(4));
- his title, and clears off any person having a prior right to the grant (rr 20 and 22);
- that he will perform his duties as administrator according to law;
- the gross and net values of the estate.

The form of oath will vary according to circumstance. The practitioner should draft the oath with care, as much of the information it should contain is a statutory requirement and omissions may require re-swearing or the filing of a fresh oath.

This book considers the three most common forms of oath, namely those for executors (probate), administration with will annexed and administration. See 3.12 for a checklist for oaths.

3.6.1 Settling documents

Practitioners may submit oaths and other documents to lead to a grant for settling by the registrar. A fee of £10.00 is charged for perusing and settling each document (Non-Contentious Probate Fees Order 1999, Fee 11 – see 3.11).

This is a useful service, particularly in complex cases. It allows the registrar to form a preliminary view of the matter and give directions at an early stage.

3.7 Executor's oath

An executor's prior right to a grant is confirmed by r 20(a). However, see 3.8.2 where a corporate body which is not a trust corporation is appointed as executor.

Form 3.7.1
Oath for executors

IN THE HIGH COURT OF JUSTICE

Family Division

In the [Principal] [District Probate] Registry

I/We

Full names (inc titles) addresses and occupations of applicants

1. ....
2. ....
3. ....
4. ....

make oath and say/do solemnly and sincerely declare and affirm that

I/we believe that

the paper writing now produced to and marked by me/us to be the true and original last

Will and codicils

will and testament [with ..... codicil(s)] of

Full names of deceased; titles of dignity or honour may be included

....

otherwise [alias name]...

of..

deceased who was born on the .... day of ....

Insert dates taken from the death certificate

..................19..../200....and

died on the ....day of ....200...

[*if the exact date of death is not known substitute*] who was last seen/known to be alive on the ......day of .... 200... and whose dead body was found on the ....day of .... 200... died *or* died on or since the ...... day of .... 200...

domiciled in England and Wales aged ..... years;

If there is land vested in the deceased which was settled previously to his death delete 'no'; give brief details of the land; the grant will be 'save and except settled land' [see 3.9.4]	that to the best of my/our knowledge, information and belief there was no land vested in the deceased which was settled previously to his death and not by his will [and codicil(s)] and which remained settled land notwithstanding his death
An executor whose appointment is not by name but by reference to a relationship should confirm that relationship	that I/we am/are the executor(s) named in the will [and codicil(s)] Notice has been given to the executors to whom power is being reserved[1]
	I/we will
*insert if there is settled land	(i) collect, get in and administer according to law the real and personal estate of the deceased [save and except settled land*] (ii) when required to do so by the court exhibit in the court a full inventory of the estate and render an account thereof to the court and (iii) when required to do so by the High Court deliver up to that Court the grant of probate;
See Table 4.1A for 'excepted estate' values *insert for 'excepted estate' cases*	to the best of my/our knowledge information and belief the gross estate passing under the grant does not exceed [excepted estate]/amounts to £........ and the net estate does not exceed [excepted estate] amounts to £........ and this is not a case in which an Inland Revenue account is required to be delivered
Alias name eg	The true name of the deceased was [Jonathan Edward Hayles] but held freehold property and a bank account in Barclays Bank in the name of [Jon Hayles] and made his will in that name
	Sworn by [applicant] at this ..... day of .... 20... Before me
	(Commissioner for Oaths)
Extracted by	[name of firm of solicitor/probate practitioner] Ref
of	[address] DX No

---

1 Notice need not be given if the executors are partners of a firm and one of the partners is applying (r 27(1A)).

3.8 Oath for administration with will annexed

This oath is prepared where no executor is named or where for some reason the executor cannot or is unable to apply to prove the will, for example, he had renounced probate, his appointment is imperfect or invalid, he has died either before or after the testator and there is no substitute appointment, etc. The prior right of the executor must be cleared. In addition, the prior right of each class mentioned in r 20 must also be cleared before a person entitled in a lower right may obtain a grant.

3.8.1 Order of priority for letters of administration with will annexed (r 20)

- Any residuary legatee or devisee holding in trust for any other person.
- Any other residuary legatee or devisee (including one for life) or where the residue is not wholly disposed by the will, any person entitled to share in the undisposed residue (including the Treasury Solicitor when claiming *bona vacantia* on behalf of the Crown) provided that:
    (a) unless a district judge or registrar otherwise directs, a residuary legatee or devisee whose legacy or devise is vested in interest shall be preferred to one entitled on the happening of a contingency; and
    (b) where the residue is not in terms wholly disposed of, the district judge or registrar may, if he is satisfied that the testator has nevertheless disposed of the whole or substantially the whole of the known estate, allow the grant to be made to any legatee or devisee entitled to, or to share in, the estate so disposed of, without regard to the persons entitled to share in any residue not disposed of by the will.
- The personal representative of any other residuary legatee or devisee (but not one for life, or holding in trust for any other person) or of any other person entitled to share in any residue not disposed of by the will.
- Any other legatee or devisee (including one for life or one holding in trust for any other person) or any creditor of the deceased, provided that, unless a district judge or registrar otherwise directs, a legatee or devisee whose legacy or devise is vested in interest shall be preferred to one entitled on the happening of a contingency.
- The personal representative of any other legatee or devisee (but not one for life or one holding in trust for any other person) or of any creditor of the deceased.

3.8.2 Corporate body (non-trust corporation) appointed executor

A corporation which is appointed sole executor is not entitled to probate as if it were an individual unless it is a trust corporation as defined in r 2(1) (by reference to s 128 of the Supreme Court Act 1981). Instead, letters of administration (with will annexed) are granted for its use and benefit and until further representation to its nominee or lawful attorney (r 36(4)(a)). The resolution appointing the nominee or the power of attorney must be presented with the application. It should contain the seal of the corporation or sufficient authentication by an authorised official. In cases of doubt, seek directions from the registrar before preparing papers.

If an individual is appointed executor together with a corporate body, their joint attorney or separately appointed attorneys applying jointly may obtain letters of administration (with will annexed) for the use and benefit of the executors. But, if the corporate body by its nominee or attorney applies alone, the right of the individual must be cleared off (r 36(4)(d)). This may be done by renunciation. The nominee or attorney of the corporate executor must confirm in the oath that the corporation is empowered by it constitution to take a grant by its nominee and a certified extract of the constitution or articles of association should be filed.

3.8.3 Form of oath

The oath for administration with will is similar to the oath for executors except that it should account for any life or minority interest (r 8(4)). A life interest or minority interest may arise by reference to a bequest in the will or upon a partial intestacy (see 3.9.2 and 3.9.3).

Form 3.8.3
Oath for administration with will

IN THE HIGH COURT OF JUSTICE

Family Division

In the [Principal] [District Probate]
Registry

I/We

Full names addresses and occupations of applicants

1. ....
2. ....
3. ....
4. ....

make oath and say/do solemnly and sincerely declare and affirm that I/we believe that

the paper writing now produced to and marked by me/us to be the true and original last

will and testament [with ..... codicil(s)] of

Full names of deceased; titles of dignity or honour may be included

....

otherwise [alias name]..

of..

Insert dates taken from the death certificate

deceased who was born on the ..... day of ....
19.../200... and

died on the .....day of ....200..

[*if the exact date of death is not known substitute*] who was last seen/known to be alive on the ..... day of .... 200... and whose dead body was found on the .... day of 200... died *or* died on or since the ..... day of .... 200...

domiciled in England and Wales aged ... years

APPLICATION FOR A GRANT OF REPRESENTATION

If there is land vested in the deceased which was settled previously to his death delete 'no'; give brief details of the land; the grant will be 'save and except settled land'	a/no life and a/no minority arises in this estate that to the best of my/our knowledge, information and belief there was no land vested in the deceased which was settled and not by his will [and codicil(s)] and which was settled previously to his death and not by his will [and codicil(s)] and which remained settled land notwithstanding his death
	A. B. the sole executor named in the will has renounced probate of the will that I/we am/are the residuary legatee(s) and devisee(s) named in the will [and codicil(s)]
	I/we will
★ Insert if there is settled land	(i) collect, get in and administer according to law the real and personal estate of the deceased [save and except settled land★]
	(ii) when required to do so by the Court exhibit in the Court a full inventory of the estate and render an account thereof to the Court and
	(iii) when required to do so by the High Court deliver up to that Court the grant of letters of administration
	to the best of my/our knowledge information and belief
	the gross estate passing under the grant does not exceed [excepted estate]/amounts to £........ and the net estate does not exceed [excepted estate]/amounts to £........
insert for 'excepted estate' cases	and this is not a case in which an Inland Revenue account is required to be delivered
Alias name, eg	The true name of the deceased was [Jonathan Edward Hayles] but held freehold property and a bank account in Barclays Bank in the name of [Jon Hayles] and made his will in that name.
	Sworn by [applicant] at this...... day of .... 20... Before me
	(Commissioner for Oaths)
Extracted by	[name of firm of solicitor/probate practitioner]
	Ref
of	[address]
	DX No

3.9 Administrator's oath

This form of oath is prepared where the deceased died wholly intestate. A grant is usually necessary to collect and administer the estate of an intestate, but if the deceased left no estate, a grant may be obtained if it is required for a special purpose, as a leading grant to another estate which the deceased was entitled to, to sue on behalf of the estate or to represent it in legal proceedings.

3.9.1 Order of priority for letters of administration (r 22)

- Lawful husband or lawful wife who has survived the deceased by 28 days (s 1(1) of the Law Reform (Succession) Act 1995)).
- Children including issue of any deceased child who died before the deceased.
- Father and mother.
- Brothers and sisters of the whole blood and issue of any such deceased brother or sister who died before the deceased.
- Brothers and sisters of the half-blood and issue of any such deceased brother or sister who died before the deceased.
- Grandparents.
- Uncles and aunts of the whole blood and issue of any such deceased uncle or aunt who died before the deceased.
- Uncles and aunts of the half blood and issue of any such uncle or aunt who died before the deceased.
- The Treasury Solicitor if he claims *bona vacantia* on behalf of the Crown.
- A creditor or a person who has no immediate beneficial interest, but may have one in the event of an accretion if all persons entitled in priority have been cleared off.

Living interest preferred

Personal representatives of persons who acquired a beneficial interest or of creditors have the same right to grants as the persons they represent. However, if there are two or more persons entitled to a grant, administration is granted to a living person in preference to a personal representative of a deceased person (rr 22(4) and 27(5)).

Description of applicants in the oath

A precise description of the applicant's must be given (see Table 3.9.1A). In the case of an intestate death before 1 January 1970, an illegitimate child should be described as the 'natural' son or daughter of the deceased. A legitimate child is described as 'lawful'. Where death occurred on or after 1 January 1970 (and before 4 April 1988), an illegitimate child has an equal right to a legitimate child (s 14 of the Family Law Reform Act 1969). However, if an illegitimate child died in the lifetime of an intestate parent, only the legitimate issue of such child may succeed to the share which their parent would have been entitled to.

Where the intestate died on or after 4 April 1988, the distinction between legitimate and illegitimate children has been removed (s 18 of the Family Law Reform Act 1987). The description of a child is 'son' or 'daughter' (Practice Direction, 19 April 1988).

3.9.2 Life interest (intestacy)

A surviving spouse is entitled in priority to a grant and may be, depending on its value, the only person entitled to the estate. A life interest arises if the deceased died leaving his spouse, and his net estate after permissible deductions exceeds the spouse's statutory legacy (see Table 3.9.2A). For example, the deceased died on 1 January 2000 intestate, leaving a lawful widow, a daughter and a son; the net estate is £250,000; after allowing for permitted deductions the widow takes absolutely £125,000 with interest (currently 6%) until payment, and a life interest in half the remainder. The daughter and son take the other half in equal shares absolutely. Upon termination of the life interest, the estate remaining passes to the children in equal shares.

Permitted deductions are:
- personal chattels as defined in s 55(1)(x) of the Administration of Estates Act 1925;
- debts;
- Inheritance Tax;
- costs, both payable and reasonably anticipated;
- probate fees;
- interest not met out of income of the estate.

The spouse may take a take a grant with one or more of the children (not exceeding three) or they may all consent to a trust corporation taking the grant. Where all the issue are minors, the spouse may nominate a fit and proper person to act jointly with her in obtaining the grant (r 32(3); see, also, 3.9.3 and Form 7.18).

Table 3.9.1A: Clearings and description on intestacy

(1) Clearing of	Description of deceased	
Spouse	swear the deceased died: a bachelor a spinster a single man[1] a single woman[1] a widower a widow	
Children or other issue	without issue	
Parents	[or] parent	
Brother or sister and their issue	[or] brother or sister of the whole [or half] blood or their issue	or any other person now entitled in priority to share in his estate by virtue of any enactment
Grandparents	[or] grandparent	
Uncles and aunts and their issue	[or] uncle or aunt of the whole [or half] blood or their issue	
(2) Applicant	Description	
Spouse	lawful husband lawful wife	and only person now entitled to the estate
Adopted child	lawful adoptive son/daughter[2]	
Adoptive parents	lawful adoptive father/mother[2]	
Adoptive brother or sister and their issue	lawful adoptive brother/sister [other] of the whole blood[2, 3]	

1 'Single' denotes that the deceased was formerly married and details of the divorce must be given in the clearing clause in the oath.

2 Succession to an intestate's estate arising as a result of an adoption order is possible where death occurred after 1 January 1950 (Adoption Act 1958); details of the adoption order including the statute under which it was made, the effect of it and confirmation that it is still subsisting must be given in the oath.

3 If the adopted person was not adopted by two spouses jointly the relationship between the adopted and other children of the adoptive parent is described as of the half-blood.

Table 3.9.2A: Statutory legacy

Death	Statutory legacy of surviving spouse	
	Issue	No issue
on or after 1 December 1993	£125,000	£200,000
between:		
1 June 1987 and 31 November 1993	£75,000	£125,000
1 March 1981 and 31 May 1987	£40,000	£85,000
15 March 1977 and 28 February 1981	£25,000	£55,000
1 July 1972 and 14 March 1977	£15,000	£40,000
1 January 1967 and 30 June 1972	£8,750	£30,000
1 January 1953 and 31 December 1966	£5,000	£20,000
1 January 1926 and 31 December 1952	£1,000	

3.9.3 Minority interest

A minor is a person who has not attained 18 years of age (s 1 of the Family Law Reform Act 1969). Where he has an interest in the estate and there are not at least two persons of full age capable and willing to apply for the grant, an application for use and benefit of a minor is made in accordance with r 32 by reference to the Children Act 1989 by:

- the father and mother of the minor if they were married to each other at the date of the birth of the minor (s 2(1)); failing which
- the mother of the minor (s 2(2)(a)); or
- the father of the minor if he acquires parental responsibility for the minor (s 4(1)); or
- the lawful adoptive parents of the minor (Pt 1, Sched 10); or
- a person in whose favour the court has made a residence order in respect of the minor (ss 8 and 12(2)); or
- a guardian of the minor either appointed or recognised (s 5 or Sched 14, paras 12, 13 or 13); or
- a local authority designated in a care order made under s 31(1)(a) of the Act; or
- a person appointed to obtain administration for the use and benefit of the minor by order of the registrar.

An application for the order is made by affidavit (see Form 7.7). It is advisable to submit a draft of the proposed affidavit in support to the registrar for perusal and comment before engrossment. At this stage, the registrar may give directions as to service of notice of the application on any other persons who may have an interest. The registrar's order should be quoted in the oath.

If there is only one person able and willing to take a grant, that person may nominate a fit and proper person for the purpose of joining him/her to take a grant for the use and benefit of the minor (r 32(3)). Generally, a fit and proper person is someone who is not under a disability, is not a bankrupt and can be relied upon to co-operate with the nominator.

3.9.4 Settled land

For the purpose of the Settled Land Act 1925, land which is or is deemed to be the subject of a settlement is settled land (s 2). Settlements were created by trust instruments (s 1) including a will of an estate owner (s 6). Land which is held on trust for sale cannot be settled land (s 1(7)). The indenture of settlement and vesting instruments together with a copy of each must be submitted with the oath. The original instruments are required for inspection and will be returned with the grant. The oath must confirm whether there was any land vested in the deceased which was settled previously to his death and not by his will and which remained settled notwithstanding his death (r 8). If any land vested in the deceased continues to remain settled after the death of the deceased, a grant of administration to the settled land is made to vest or convey the land to the next tenant.

The order of priority for the grant is set out in r 29(2):
- special executors – the persons who are the trustees of the settlement at the date of a testator's death and as such are either appointed as special executors in the will or, in default of appointment, are deemed to be appointed;
- the trustees of the settlement at the date of the grant;
- the personal representatives of the deceased (the previous tenant for life).

A grant to settled land will be one of letters of administration and the grant to the free estate of the deceased will expressly be save and except land. It is advisable to lodge the indenture or instrument of settlement, the vesting deed and a draft oath for examination by the registrar and his confirmation that a grant to settled land is necessary. If the settlement was created by a will, an office copy of the will should be submitted.

3.9.4.1 The Trusts of Land and Appointment of Trustees Act 1996

This Act came into force on 1 January 1997. It will eventually phase out strict settlements made under the Settled Land Act 1925. Part 1 of the new Act replaces the previous system of setting up trusts for sale and strict settlements. Under s 1 of the Act, any trust of property which consists of or includes land is called 'trust of land'. While it is not now possible to create new settlements under the Settled Land Act 1925, the new Act expressly excludes existing settlements which were in force at its commencement. Such settlements may be altered or re-settled within the powers contained in the settlements. Consequently, for the foreseeable future there will continue to be a need for settled land grants.

3.9.5 Oath for administration

The contents of this oath will depend on the circumstance of each case. As with an oath for letters of administration with will, a statement as to life and minority interests must be included (r 8(4)). The oath must show clearly how persons with a prior interest have been cleared off down to the applicant (see Table 3.9.1A).

Form 3.9.5

Oath for administrators

IN THE HIGH COURT OF JUSTICE

Family Division

In the [Principal] [District Probate] Registry

I/We

Full names addresses and occupations of applicants

1. ....
2. ....
3. ....
4. ....

make oath and say/do solemnly and sincerely declare and affirm that

Full names of deceased; titles of dignity or honour may be included	.... otherwise..[alias name]................... of..
Insert dates taken from the death certificate	deceased who was born on the ..... day of .... 19.../200... and died on the ..... day of .... 200... [*if the exact date of death is not known substitute*] who was last seen/known to be alive on the ..... day of .... 200... and whose dead body was found on the .... 200... died or died on or since the ..... day of .... 200...
See Table 3.91A for wording of clearing	domiciled in England and Wales intestate aged ... years [*insert clearing*]
If there is land vested in the deceased which was settled previously to his death delete 'no'; give brief details of the land; the grant will be 'save and except settled land'	a/no life and a/no minority arises in this estate under the intestacy to the best of my/our knowledge, information vested in the and belief there was no land vested in the deceased which was settled previously to his death and which remained settled land notwithstanding his death
See Table 3.9.1A for wording of title	I/we am/are the I/we will (i) collect, get in and administer according to law the real and personal estate of the deceased [save and except settled land] (ii) when required to do so by the Court exhibit in the Court a full inventory of the estate and render an account thereof to the Court and (iii) when required to do so by the High Court deliver up to that Court the grant of letters of administration to the best of my/our knowledge information and belief
See Table 4.1A for estates' values appropriate to excepted estates	the gross estate passing under the grant does not exceed [excepted estate]/amounts to £......... and the net estate does not exceed [excepted estate]/ amounts to £.........
Insert for 'excepted estate' cases	and this is not a case in which an Inland Revenue account is required to be delivered

Alias name, eg	The true name of the deceased was [Jonathan Edward Hayles] but held freehold property and a bank account in Barclays Bank in the name of [Jon Hayles]
	Sworn by [applicant] at this ..... day of.......... 20... Before me
	(Commissioner for Oaths)
Extracted by	[name of firm of solicitor/probate practitioner]
	Ref
of	[address]
	DX No

3.10 Foreign domicile

The normal rules of priority are suspended where the deceased died domiciled outside England and Wales. The practice and procedure for an application for a grant of representation in this case is governed by r 30.

Subject to two exceptions, a grant of administration (with will annexed, where appropriate) is made upon an order being made by the court to:

- *the person entrusted with the administration of the estate of the deceased by the court having jurisdiction at the place where he died domiciled* (r 30(1)(a)) – the original entrusting document or a copy sealed and/or certified by the court which made it must be produced. For it to be acceptable as such, the entrusting document should be similar to an English grant. That is, it should on the face of it confer administration of the whole estate or authority to collect the estate of the deceased and pay debts and distribute. If there is a will, a copy of it should be annexed to the entrusting document or failing this, it must be obvious that the will which the applicant wishes to prove is the one referred to in the document. The person entrusted does not have to clear off an executor named in the will;
- *(where no one is entrusted) the person beneficially entitled to the estate of the deceased by the laws of the place where the deceased died domiciled* (r 30(1)(b)) – an affidavit of law or a notarial certificate or act by an notary practising in the country where the deceased died domiciled will establish this fact (r 19). If the deceased made a will, the evidence must also confirm its validity. However, if a court in that country has issued an order, decree or other act of succession or heirship,

this should be placed before the registrar for consideration. A decree of succession of a foreign court of an order confirming the rights of kin or a residuary or other beneficiary named in a will is usually sufficient to confirm the beneficial entitlement of that person. If more than one person is beneficially entitled to the estate, the registrar may direct whether one or more or which of those persons should join in the application. It is advisable to seek directions before preparing papers in support of the application for order. Again, a person who is beneficially entitled does not have to clear off an executor named in the will of the deceased;

- *such persons as the registrar may direct* (r 30(1)(c)) – this is a discretionary exercise of the registrar's jurisdiction which may be used in a variety of circumstances. Common examples are: the deceased left no estate in the country of domicile and a grant is not required there; the person entitled in priority has died without taking a grant and his heirs wish to take a grant; proceeding in respect of the deceased's estate are pending in the country of domicile and grant is necessary here to prevent loss to the estate, etc. A full statement of the facts should be placed before the registrar so that appropriate directions can be given.

It is often the case that parties abroad send to practitioners in this country papers which purport to entrust administration or confer beneficial entitlement. It is advisable that these papers, together with translations where necessary, are referred to a registrar at an early stage for his comment and direction as to their suitability.

A translation of a document in a foreign language should normally be notarial or be authenticated by an affidavit of the translator setting out his qualification to translate and confirming that the translation is complete and accurate. Other translations, such as those prepared by a translation service of a foreign court or government may be considered.

The exceptions referred to earlier for which orders of the court are not necessary to lead to a grant are:
- *probate of any will which is admissible to proof* (r 30(3)(a)) – application may be made by the executor if the will is in English or Welsh or the executor according to tenor if the will is in a foreign language. An appointment in a foreign language purporting to mean 'executor' is not accepted by the courts in England and Wales. A will is accepted as admissible to proof if its validity has been established. This may be by a decree or order in favour of the will by the court of domicile or a notarial act either making or publishing the will or an affidavit of law. A will in English executed in England and Wales under s 9

of the Wills Act 1837 is admissible by reference to s 1 of the Wills Act 1963. Its execution conforms to the internal law in force in the territory where it was executed;

- *where the whole or substantially the whole of the estate in England and Wales consists of immovables, a grant in respect of the whole estate may be made in accordance with the law which would have been applicable if the deceased had died domiciled in England and Wales* – under this provision, the court may override the entitlement in respect of movables of the person entrusted or beneficially entitled.

3.10.1 Oath by person entrusted (r 30(1)(a))

The oath must be submitted with the original entrusting document or a sealed and certified copy which has been issued by the court which made the original grant or entrusting document.

Form 3.10.1
Oath for letters of administration [with will] r 30(1)(a)

(This form should be adapted for an oath for letters of administration)

IN THE HIGH COURT OF JUSTICE

Family Division

In the [Principal] [District Probate] Registry

I/We

Full names addresses and occupations of applicants

1. ....
2. ....
3. ....
4. ....

make oath and say/do solemnly and sincerely declare and affirm that
I/we believe that
the paper writing now produced to and marked by me/us to be the true and original last

will and testament [with codicil(s)]

Full names of deceased; titles of dignity or honour may be included

of
....
otherwise..[alias name].......................................
of..

Insert dates taken from the death certificate

deceased who was born on the ..... day of ....
19.../200... and died on the ..... day ....
200..
[*if the exact date of death is not known substitute*] who was last seen/known to be alive on the ...... day of .... 200.... and whose dead body was found on the ..... day of .... 200... died or died on or since the ..... day of .... 200...
domiciled in [state] aged ... years

If there is land vested in the deceased which was settled previously to his death delete 'no'; give brief details of the land; the grant will be 'save and except settled land'

a/no life and a/no minority arises in this estate that to the best of my/our knowledge, information and belief there was no land vested in deceased which was settled previously to his death and not by his will [and codicil(s)] and which remained settled land notwithstanding his death

I am/we are the person(s) entrusted with the administration of the estate of the deceased by the court which has jurisdiction at the place where the deceased died domiciled

I/we hereby apply for an order under r 30(1)(a) of the Non-Contentious Probate Rules 1987 directing that letters of administration [with will annexed]of the estate of the deceased be granted to me/us
I/we will
(i) collect, get in and administer according to law the real and personal estate of the deceased [save and except settled land]
(ii) when required to do so by the Court exhibit in the Court a full inventory of the estate and render an account thereof to the Court and

(iii) when required to do so by the High Court deliver up to that Court the grant of letters of administration to the best of my/our knowledge information and belief

Form D18 controlled by the CTO must be filed and the gross estate passing under the grant amounts to £........ and the net estate amounts to £........

If the deceased was known by various names state his true name and if held assets in alias names confirm this by stating at least one asset held in each name (see Form 3.9.5)

Sworn by [applicant] at this ..... day of   20...
Before me

(Commissioner for Oaths)

Extracted by   [name of firm of solicitor/probate practitioner]

                  Ref
of   [address]
                  DX No

3.10.2 Oath by person beneficially entitled (r 30(1)(b))

An affidavit of law or a notarial certificate confirming the applicant's entitlement together with an affidavit of facts should be filed with the oath. Alternatively, the affidavit of facts may be incorporated in the oath.

Form 3.10.2

Rule 30(1)(b)

Oath for letters of administration with will annexed

(*This form should be adapted for an oath for letter of administration*)

IN THE HIGH COURT OF JUSTICE

Family Division

In the [Principal] [District Probate] Registry

I/We

Full names addresses and occupations of applicants

1. ....
2. ....
3. ....
4. ....

make oath and say/do solemnly and sincerely declare and affirm that

I/we believe that

the paper writing now produced to and marked by me/us to be the true and original last

will and testament [with codicil(s)] of

Full names of deceased; titles of dignity or honour may be included

....

otherwise..[alias name]..

of..

Insert dates taken from the death certificate

deceased who was born on the ..... day of .... 19.../200... and died on the ..... day .... 200..

[*if the exact date of death is not known substitute*] who was last seen/known to be alive on the ...... day of .... 200... and whose dead body was found on the ..... day of .... 200... died or died on or since the ..... day of .... 200...

domiciled in [state] aged ... years

APPLICATION FOR A GRANT OF REPRESENTATION

If there is land vested in the deceased which was settled previously to his death delete 'no'; give brief details of the land; the grant will be 'save and except settled land'	a/no life and a/no minority arises in this estate that to the best of my/our knowledge, information and belief there was no land vested in the deceased which was settled previously to his death and not by his will [and codicil(s)] and which remained settled land notwithstanding his death
If the court of domicile has issued a decree of inheritance or final order which confirms the entitlement of the applicant(s) exhibit the original or official copy	No one has been entrusted with the administration of the estate of the deceased by the court having jurisdiction at the place where the deceased died domiciled
	I am/we are the person(s) beneficially entitled to the estate of the deceased by the laws of the place where the deceased died domiciled
If an affidavit of law or notarial certificate is being lodged confirm those matters of fact which the expert relies on to form his opinion, eg, names and relationship of kin to the deceased, nationality, etc	I/we hereby apply for an order under r 30(1)(b) of the Non-Contentious Probate Rules 1987 directing that letters of administration [with will annexed] of the estate of the deceased be granted to me/us
	I/we will
	(i) collect, get in and administer according to law the real and personal estate of the deceased [save and except settled land]
	(ii) when required to do so by the Court exhibit in the Court a full inventory of the estate and render an account thereof to the Court and
	(iii) when required to do so by the High Court deliver up to that Court the grant of letters of administration
	to the best of my/our knowledge information and belief
Form D18 controlled by the CTO must be filed	and the gross estate passing under the grant amounts to £......... and the net estate amounts to £.........
If the deceased was known by various names state his true name and if held assets in alias names confirm this by stating at least one asset held in each name (see Form 3.9.5)	

	Sworn by [applicant] at this ..... day of ....20...
	Before me
	(Commissioner for Oaths)
Extracted by	[name of firm of solicitor/probate practitioner]
	Ref
of	[address]
	DX No

3.10.3 Oath following discretionary order (r 30(1)(c))

This oath is prepared after an order is made under the rule; the application for the order is made separately by an affidavit of facts which sets out the circumstances why the applicant seeks to override the entitlement of the persons entrusted or beneficially entitled or other matters as directed previously by the registrar.

Form 3.10.3

Oath for letters of administration

(r 30(1)(c))

(This form may be adapted for an oath for letters of administration)

IN THE HIGH COURT OF JUSTICE

Family Division

In the [Principal] [District Probate]
Registry

I/We

Full names addresses and occupations of applicants	1. ....
	2. ....
	3. ....
	4. ....

make oath and say/do solemnly and sincerely declare and affirm that

I/we believe that the paper writing now produced to and marked by me/us to be the true and original will and testament [with codicil(s)] of

Full names of deceased; titles of dignity or honour may be included

....

otherwise..[alias name]..

of...

Insert dates taken from the death certificate

deceased who was born on the ..... day of .... 19.../200... and died on the ..... day .... 200..

[*if the exact date of death is not known substitute*] who was last seen/known to be alive on the ...... day of .... 200... and whose dead body was found on the ..... day of .... 200... died or died on or since the ..... day of .... 200...

domiciled in [state] aged ... years

If there is land vested in the deceased which was settled previously to his death delete 'no'; give brief details of the land; the grant will be 'save and except settled land'

a/no life and a/no minority arises in this estate that to the best of my/our knowledge, information and belief there was no land vested in the deceased which was settled previously to his death and not by his will [and codicil(s)] and which remained settled land notwithstanding his death

On the ..... day of .... 20... it was ordered by Mr District Registrar of this Division that letters of administration (with will annexed) be granted to me/us by virtue of r 30(1)(c) of the Non-Contentious Probate Rules 1987

I/we will

(i) collect, get in and administer according to law the real and personal estate of the deceased [save and except settled land]

(ii) when required to do so by the Court exhibit in the Court a full inventory of the estate and render an account thereof to the Court and

(iii) when required to do so by the High Court deliver up to that Court the grant of letters of administration

to the best of my/our knowledge information and belief

Form D18 controlled by the CTO must be filed

the gross estate passing under the grant amounts to £........ and the net estate amounts to £........

If the deceased was known by various names state his true name and if held assets in alias names confirm this by stating at least one asset held in each name (see Form 3.9.5)

Sworn by [applicant] at this ..... day of ....20...
Before me

(Commissioner for Oaths)

Extracted by   [name of firm of solicitor/probate practitioner]

Ref

of   [address]

DX No

3.11 Non-Contentious Probate fees

Probate fees are payable in accordance with the Non-Contentious Probate Fees Order 1999 SI 1999/688.

Table 3.11A
Non-Contentious Probate Fees

Fee no		Fee
	Application for a grant	
1	On an application for a grant (or for re-sealing a grant) other than an application to which fee no 3 applies, where the assessed value of the estate exceeds £5,000	£50

Personal application

2   Where the application under fee 1 is made by a personal applicant (not being an application to which fee no 3 applies) and where the assessed value of the estate exceeds £5,000 fee no 2 is payable in addition   £80

Special applications

3   For a duplicate or second or subsequent grant (including one following a revoked grant) in respect of the same deceased person, other than a grant preceded only by a grant limited to settled land, to trust property or to part of the estate   £15

Caveats

4   For the entry or extension of a caveat   £15

Search

5   On an application of a standing search to be carried out in an estate, for each period of six months including the issue of a copy grant and will, if any (irrespective of the number of pages)   £5

Deposit of wills

6   On depositing a will for safe custody in the principal registry or a district registry   £15

Inspection

7   On inspection of any will or other document retained in the registry (in the presence of an officer of the registry)   £15

Copy documents

8   On the request for a copy of any document whether or not provided as a certified copy:
    (a) for the first copy   £5

(b) for every subsequent copy of the same document if supplied at the same time[2] £1

(c) where copies of any document are made available on a computer disk or in any other electronic form, for each such copy £3

(d) where the search for the index is required, in addition to fee no 8(a), (b) or (c) as appropriate for each period of 4 years searched after the first 4 years £3

Oaths

9 Except on a personal application for a grant, for administering an oath,

9.1 for each deponent to each affidavit £5

9.2 for marking each exhibit £2

Determination of costs

10 For determining costs
[The same fees as are payable from time to time for determining costs under the Supreme Court Fees Order 1999, (the relevant fees are set out in fee 10 in Sched 1 to that Order)]

Settling documents

11 For perusing and settling citations, advertisements, oaths, affidavits, or other documents, for each document settled £10

---

[2] Includes a copy of a grant or will requested on application for the grant.

3.12 Checklist for oaths

The oath will be returned for re-swearing if the following matters or any of them are omitted:

- *Names of applicant or deceased* – if the name of an applicant executor or applicant beneficiary is incorrectly given in the will, an affidavit of identity should be filed with the oath (see Form 7.6). Examples of incorrect names used are 'Christopher Jones' where the correct name is 'Paul Christopher Jones'. If a medial name is not included in the will, the oath should include the statement 'in the will called ...' after the name of the applicant.

- *Domicile of the deceased* – if the deceased died in a territory such as the UK, the US or Australia, where each State or country has its own system of internal law, the oath must confirm the particular State or country in which the deceased died domiciled.
- *Title and clearing* (see 3.9.1 and Table 3.9.1A)
  (a) probate/administration with will – executor or residuary beneficiary has not accounted for and his renunciation had not been filed; title omitted from the oath;
  (b) administration – status of intestate, for example, 'a widow', 'intestate' omitted;
  (c) title of applicant is incomplete, for example, '*lawful* widow', 'brother of *the whole blood*', etc;
  (d) incomplete clearing: omission of a class such as brothers and sisters of the whole blood where a nephew of the whole blood applies without confirming through whom he takes his title. This defect may be remedied by including the complete clearing or combining the clearing with the title, for example: 'I am a nephew of the whole blood and one of the persons entitled to share in the estate of the deceased, being the son of Gill Butler a sister of the whole blood of the deceased who died in her lifetime.'
- *Details of divorce* – the oath should state the date of the divorce and the court which granted it. The oath must be re-sworn unless it states that the deceased died a single person, in which case a copy of the decree absolute may be produced instead.
- *Settled land and minority and life interest clauses* – see 3.9.3 and 3.9.4.
- *Codicil not referred to in the oath* – nor marked in accordance with r 10.

The omission of the following matters may be remedied by the certificate on the oath or separately by a partner in the practitioner's firm:

- *true name of deceased*;
- *address of the deceased/applicant*;
- *date of death* and produce a copy of the death certificate;
- *alias name* – certificate to specify at least one asset in the alias name;
- *limitation of an attorney*;

- *statement that Inland Revenue account not required to be delivered* in 'excepted estate' cases (see 4.2);
- *notice to executors having power reserved*;
- *widow's statutory entitlement* – intestacy – on a widow's application if the oath does confirm that the net value of the estate after permitted deduction does/does not exceed the statutory threshold and that she is the only person entitled/now entitled (see 3.9.2 and Table 3.9.2A).

3.13 Papers to be lodged in a grant application

Administration – oath, renunciations (if any), if the estate is not an 'excepted estate', Form D18 either endorsed by the Capital Taxes Office that Inheritance Tax has been paid, or certified by practitioner under the self-assessment procedure that no tax is payable, and probate fees.

Administration with will – oath, will including codicils (all marked by applicant and commissioner), affidavits of execution, identity, etc, if appropriate, renunciations (if any), Form D18 (see administration above) and probate fee.

Probate – oath, will including codicils (all marked by applicant and commissioner), affidavits of execution, identity, etc, if appropriate, renunciations (if any), Form D18 (see administration, above) and probate fee.

These lists are not exhaustive. The requirement for other papers to be submitted will depend on the circumstances of each case. This will be confirmed by the probate registry on a preliminary inquiry.

4 The Inland Revenue Account

4.1 The Inland Revenue account

The requirement for delivery of an Inland Revenue account prior to the grant being made is governed by s 109 of the Supreme Court Act 1981. The Act also provides for arrangements to be made between the President of the Family Division and the Commissioners of the Inland Revenue to dispense with the delivery of accounts in certain cases (s 109(2), and see 4.2).

4.2 Excepted estates

These are estates which fall within the definition of the Inheritance Tax (Delivery of Accounts) Regulations 2000 SI 2000/967 for which delivery of an account prior to grant being issued may be dispensed with. The Commissioners of the Inland Revenue are empowered to make these regulations by the Inheritance Act 1984. The current Regulations amend and update previous regulations which have been made from time to time to reflect general changes to the value of estates in line with inflation.

Thus, in respects of deaths on or after 1 August 1981, an account is not required to be delivered before the grant issues if:
- the gross value does not exceed the value given in Table 4.1A below;
- the estate comprises only property which passes by will or intestacy, under a nomination or survivorship in a joint beneficial tenancy;
- the value of the estate outside the UK does not exceed the value given in Table 4.1B;
- the deceased died in the UK; and

- the deceased made no simple lifetime transfers exceeding the limits set out in Table 4.1C chargeable to Inheritance Tax or Capital Transfer Tax.

Table 4.1A 'Excepted estate' values for oath

Gross not exceeding	*Death on or after*
£210,000	6 April 2000
£200,000	6 April 1998
£180,000	6 April 1996
£145,000	6 April 1995
£125,000	1 April 1991
£115,000	1 April 1990
£100,000	1 April 1989
£70,000	1 April 1987
£40,000	1 April 1983
£25,000	1 April 1981
Net estate (for calculation of probate fee)	
Not exceeding £5,000	No fee
Not exceeding gross value relevant to date of death (see above)	£50

Table 4.1B Value of estate outside the UK

Death on or after	*Value*
6 April 1998	£50,000
6 April 1996	£30,000
1 April 1989	£15,000
1 April 1987	£10,000
1 April 1983	£2,000 *
1 April 1981	£1,000 *
* or 10% of the estate, whichever is the higher figure	

Table 4.1C Lifetime transfers such as cash or quoted securities and shares

Deaths on or after	Value of transfer not exceeding
6 April 2000	£75,000
6 April 1998	£50,000
6 April 1996	£30,000

An estate cannot be 'excepted' if:
- the deceased had an interest in settled property;
- the deceased made lifetime transfers which became liable for tax due to his death within seven years thereafter;
- the deceased made a gift with reservation which subsisted up to or within seven years of his death.

Subsequent delivery of account

The regulations allow the Inland Revenue to call for an account by notice in writing within 35 days of the date of the grant provided that it is not a limited grant.

4.3 Forms of account (deaths on or after 18 March 1986)

A new Form IHT200 was introduced in April 2000. This Form, together with supplementary pages D1–D18 has replaced all previous forms with the exception of Form A5-C (submitted when application is made for a second grant). The forms should be completed with the use of the Guide IHT210 and Notes for Supplementary pages SP2. The forms are designed for self-assessment by practitioners and Guide IHT213 are notes for working out any Inheritance Tax payable using a work sheet IHT (WS) provided in the forms pack.

If Inheritance Tax is payable, the account is submitted to the Capital Taxes Office together with the IHT200 including the Probate Summary which is endorsed as to tax paid and returned together with a tax receipt to the practitioner. The D18 is filed in the probate registry together with probate papers as proof of tax paid and that the Commissioners for the Inland Revenue have no objection to a grant being issued. The Inheritance Tax forms are usually passed on a provisional basis to enable a grant to issue, but the account is re-examined in detail after the grant. A completed specimen form is reproduced in Chapter 7.

IHT200 is used in all cases irrespective of whether the deceased died domiciled in or outside the UK. Supplementary page D2 should be completed if the deceased died domiciled outside the UK.

IHT200 is not used for deaths which have occurred before 18 March 1986. In these cases, the appropriate forms should be obtained from the Capital Taxes Office (see Chapter 9 for address).

Form A5-C should be used when the application is for:
- a grant of double probate
- a grant *de bonis non administratis*;
- a grant following a cessate grant.

4.4 Delivery and payment of Inheritance Tax

The account of the estate must be delivered by the personal representatives within 12 months after the last day of the month in which death occurred or within three months from acting (s 216(6)(a) of the Inheritance Tax Act 1984). The account must include all the estate to which the deceased was beneficially entitled. If the whole estate cannot be ascertained, and it is known that the final value will exceed the threshold for payment of Inheritance Tax, the practitioner should refer to the Capital Taxes Office before making the application.

Tax is payable six months after the end of the month in which death occurred unless it is being paid by instalments (ss 227–29 of the Inheritance Tax Act 1984). Categories of property on which Inheritance Tax may be paid by instalments include:
- land;
- shares and securities owned by the deceased which gave him control of a company;
- unquoted shares whose value exceeds £20,000 and the nominal value is not less than 10% of all the shares in the company or if ordinary shares, the nominal value is not less than 10% of all ordinary shares of the company at the date of death;
- shares unquoted or listed on the Unlisted Securities Market and not less than 20% of tax payable is attributable to the shares or other property with the instalment option;

- business interest including a business carried out in the exercise of a profession or vocation; a business which is not carried on for gain is not included;
- woodlands.

4.5 Threshold for and rate of Inheritance Tax (1989 onwards)

The rate of tax for the estate which exceeds the threshold is 40%. The threshold for tax is raised periodically by Inheritance Tax Indexation Orders:

- 6 April 1989, £118,000: SI 1989/481;
- 6 April 1990, £128,000: SI 1990/680;
- 6 April 1991, £140,000: SI 1991/735;
- 10 March 1992, £150,000: SI 1992/625;
- 6 April 1995, £154,000: SI 1994/3011;
- 6 April 1996, £200,000: s 183 of the Finance Act 1996;
- 6 April 1997, £215,000: s 93 of the Finance Act 1997;
- 6 April 1998, £223,000: SI 1998/756;
- 6 April 1999, £231,000: SI 1999/596;
- 6 April 2000, £234,000: SI 2000/803.

5 Disputes and Impediments to the Making of a Grant

5.1 Caveats (r 44)

Any person who wishes to prevent issue of a grant without notice to himself may enter a caveat in any registry or sub-registry (r 44(1)). However, the caveat will not prevent the court from granting administration pending a probate claim (s 117 of the Supreme Court Act 1981) or a grant *ad colligenda bona*. Moreover, a caveat will not prevent a grant from being issued on the day the caveat is entered or if the grant is to the caveator himself.

The caveat is entered by notice in Form 3 (Non-Contentious Probate Rules 1987 (see Form 7.13). The caveator may attend the probate registry or sub-registry personally and complete Form 3 (r 44(2)(a)), or he may send it at his own risk by post to any registry or sub-registry (r 44(2)(b)). The caveator should ensure that the correct name and any alias names are given and, if the deceased died in the UK, his name and date of death as recorded in the register of deaths should be included in the caveat (District Judges' Practice Direction, 12 January 1999). On receipt of the caveat, it is entered in the probate computer system and searched against all pending applications. The caveat will not prevent a grant from being issued under a variant of the name entered. For example, a caveat is entered in the name of Stephen Barrie Meeks and a grant subsequently issues in the name of Steven Barry Meekes. A range of dates may be given if the caveator is uncertain of the date of death.

The caveat remains in force for six months and it may be extended successively for further periods of six months by written application for its renewal (r 44(3)(a)). The application for extension must be lodged in the last month of the initial or previous six month period.

A caveat may be withdrawn by the caveator at any time provided that he has not entered an appearance to a warning (r 44(11)).

5.2 Central index of pending applications and caveats

A central index of every pending application and every caveat which the Senior District Judge is obliged to keep (rr 44(4) and 57) is maintained in the probate computer system. Leeds District Probate Registry is the nominated registry for the purpose of r 44 and some formalities concerning caveats, such as a warning to a caveat and the entry of an appearance, must be directed to the registrar at that registry.

5.3 Reasons for entering a caveat

- As a preliminary to issuing a probate claim in the Chancery Division or commencing proceedings in a county court and to allow the caveator sufficient time to obtain legal advice or gather evidence.
- The caveator may wish to declare a contrary interest to a declared or proposed applicant.
- The caveator wishes to show cause why a grant should not issue to a particular person.
- As a preliminary to issuing a citation.

5.4 Sequence of steps following the entry of a caveat

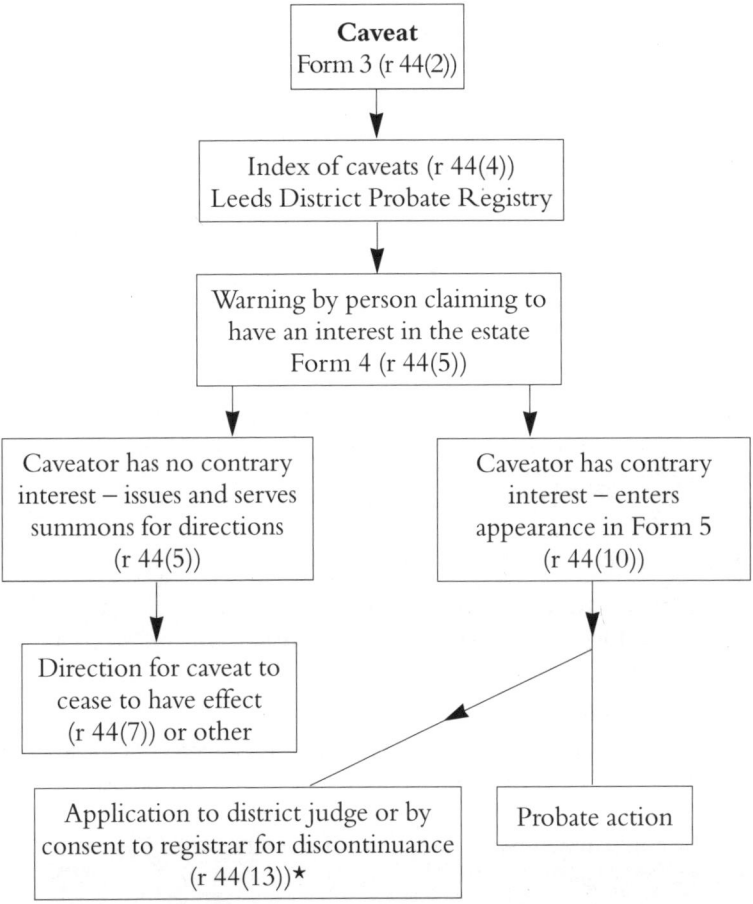

*usual if following the filing of an appearance, no contrary interest is disclosed.

NOTE:
(i) A caveat may be withdrawn at any time if no appearance has been filed (r 44(11)).
(ii) The caveat ceases to have effect if a caveator takes no steps within eight days of service of a warning on him and the person warning files an affidavit in the Leeds District Probate Registry confirming such service and that no summons for directions has been issued.

5.5 Warning and appearance

A warning is a notice in Form 4 (Non-Contentious Probate Rules 1987) (see Form 7.14) by any person who has an interest in the estate, including a person whose application has been stopped by the entry of the caveat. It warns the caveator to take either of the following steps within eight days (including the day of service of the notice):

- enter an appearance at the nominated registry (Leeds District Probate Registry) setting out his contrary interest to that of the person warning (r 44(5)); or
- if he does not have a contrary interest but he objects to a grant being made to the person warning to issue and serve a summons for directions by a registrar at any probate registry (in the Principal Registry by a district judge)(r 44(6)).

An appearance is entered by completing Form 5 (Non-Contentious Probate Rules 1987) (see Form 7.17) and filing it in the nominated registry (Leeds) and serving a copy of it on the person warning (r 44(10)).

A caveat in respect of which an appearance is entered remains in force until probate proceedings are begun or the parties apply to discontinue the caveat by consent (r 44(13)).

Alternatively, if the caveator does not have a contrary interest, but he opposes the issue of a grant to the person warning or any proposed applicant, he may file a summons for directions (see 5.8).

A caveator may withdraw his caveat at any time if he has not entered an appearance to a warning (r 44(11)), but if the caveator takes no steps in answer to a warning, the person warning may at any time after eight days of service of the warning file an affidavit in the nominated registry (Leeds) confirming service of the warning and the caveat ceases to have effect (r 44(12)).

5.6 Probate claims

Following the implementation of the Civil Procedure Rules 1998 (on 26 April 1999), probate proceedings have replaced probate action and these are begun by a probate claim. A probate claim may be started in the Chancery Division at the Royal Courts of Justice in London or at a Chancery District Registry. Alternatively, if the value of the estate does not exceed the current county court limit of £30,000, the claim may be filed in a county court. On the commencement of a probate claim, the Chancery Court or county court advises the Senior District

Judge of the proceedings through Leeds District Probate Registry, who then notifies every caveator who is not a claimant in the proceedings. The probate claim prevents a grant being issued until the determination of the claim. An exception to this is a grant pending claim under s 117 of the Supreme Court Act 1981, or following an order of a district judge of the Principal Registry made on summons (r 45(3)).

Note that any caveats entered after the determination of the probate claim or in respect of which notice of the claim has not been given (under r 45(1)) continue to remain in force.

5.7 Citations

A basic guide to citations is set out here. A more detailed discussion will be found in *Tristram and Coote's Probate Practice*, 28th edn.

A citation is an instrument under seal of the court which requires a named person:

- to accept or refuse a grant to which he is entitled (r 47(1)) – a person with an inferior right such as a legatee named in a will or a creditor of an intestate cites all persons with a prior right who have not renounced;
- to obtain a grant of probate (r 47(3)) – a person interested in the estate cites an executor who has intermeddled in the estate without proving the will and six months have elapsed since the date of death;
- to propound a will (r 48) – an applicant for a grant who has knowledge of a purported will (which he believes to be invalid) and whose rights may be affected, should cite any executors and other persons interested under such a will to propound it.

5.7.1 Practice in citations

The practitioner should first lodge a draft citation together with a draft supporting affidavit for settling by the registrar. Any will which is to be referred in the citation should also be submitted with the papers. If the will is not in the proposed citor's possession and the person who has it refuses to lodge it with the registry in which the citation is being issued, the proposed citor should first issue a subpoena to bring in the will (r 50(1)). However, if the registrar is satisfied that it is impracticable to require the will to be lodged, he has power to dispense with this requirement.

The citation may issue out of any registry (r 46(1)) and the citor should enter a caveat before issuing the citation (r 50(1)).

5.7.2 Service of citation and subsequent procedure

The citation should be served personally unless the registrar directs some other mode of service, including notice by advertisement (r 46(4)). Service by advertisement is used when a citor such as a creditor of an intestate wishes to cite kin whose identity or whose whereabouts are unknown.

If the person cited to accept or refuse a grant, or being an executor to whom power is reserved does not file an appearance after he receives the citation or after service of it in accordance with the registrar's direction, the citor may apply without notice by affidavit for an order for a grant to himself or for a declaration that the rights of an executor have wholly ceased (r 47(5)(a) and (c)). This application should also be supported by an affidavit of service of the citation (r 47(6)).

If an intermeddling executor who is cited does not enter an appearance, or any person cited enters an appearance but does not issue proceedings with due diligence, the citor may issue and serve a summons (see 5.8 for practice) for an order for a grant to himself or some other person specified in the summons or for the existing grant to be endorsed to the effect that the rights of an executor to whom power is reserved have ceased (r 47(5)(b) and (7)).

5.8 Issuing a summons

The practitioner prepares the summons in duplicate (see Form 7.17) and sends it to the probate registry where it is to be heard (r 61). This is usually the registry in which an application for a grant is pending, a grant is issued, a caveat is entered or a citation is filed.

A summons which is to be heard by a judge or district judge should be sent to the probate department in the Principal Registry. The practitioner must note the summons with a time estimate and whether counsel is attending the hearing. The registry will endorse the summons with the date, time and place and return a sealed copy to the practitioner for service as prescribed by r 66(2). This requires that if the summons is to be served on any person, it should be served at least two clear days before the hearing date. For the purpose of service, Saturdays, Sundays and public holidays are not included. The registrar may direct which other persons are to be served.

5.9 Standing search

A person who does not wish to prevent the sealing of a grant, but wishes to know when it issues, may make an application for a standing search (r 43 and Form 2, Non-Contentious Probate Rules 1987). The application in the prescribed form (see 7.16) is sent to any registry or sub-registry with the fee (£15). All alternative names for the deceased should be included in the form. Upon searching, the registry will send to the applicant an office copy of any grant of representation and any will of a deceased whose description matches that given in the application and which grant was issued not more than 12 months before the date of receipt of the application or issued within six months after that date (r 43). The application for the standing search may be extended upon written application and payment of a further fee.

The standing search procedure is useful where a person wishes to be informed of the issue of a grant so that he can commence proceedings against the personal representatives of the deceased.

6 Administration of the Estate

6.1 Priority for debts and liabilities

After the grant has been issued to him, the personal representative is concerned with the administration of the estate. The payment of funeral expenses, debts and liabilities of the deceased is a first charge on the deceased's estate (s 32(1) of the Administration of Estates Act 1925 (the Act)). The liability of the personal representative is confined to the assets which come into his possession which the deceased was entitled to as the beneficial owner. In an intestacy, the personal representative holds the estate on trust for sale and to convert into money any part of it which does not consist of money (s 33(1) of the Act). He is liable for all the debts of the deceased for which there are sufficient assets to pay.

Note that children no longer have to bring lifetime advances into account against their entitlement on intestacy, nor do a surviving spouse and children have to bring gifts given by will against such entitlement (s 1(2) of the Law Reform (Succession) Act 1995).

6.2 The practitioner's role

The practitioner will have ascertained known debts of the deceased when he prepared the probate papers for the grant. He may protect the personal representative from liability for any unknown debts by giving notice to the persons interested by advertising in accordance with s 27(1) of the Trustee Act 1925 (see Forms 7.21 and 7.22). The advertisement should be placed without delay in the *London Gazette* and a newspaper which has a circulation in the district where any land belonging to the deceased is situated and, depending on the circumstances of the case, anywhere where a court in an administration action would have directed.

Note that an executor may advertise before obtaining probate, but an administrator must first obtain administration (following the principles of vesting of a deceased's estate, as discussed earlier). The notice is directed 'to persons interested' (*Re Aldhous* [1955] 2 All ER 80) and it must allow persons interested in the estate to respond no less than two months from the date of the advertisement. Thus, the effect of the notice is to give the personal representative the same protection as a court order, but it does not absolve him from any claim made during this period which is not in answer to the advertisement.

In addition, it does not prevent a person who is claiming from 'following' the trust property, that is, pursuing his claims against beneficiaries who have received the property (s 27(2) of the Trustee Act 1925).

Where it is impractical to advertise, the practitioner should apply to the court (under the Civil Procedure Rules, Sched 1, r 85.2) for an order for leave to distribute the estate on the footing that all debts have been ascertained (*Re Gess* [1942] Ch 33), or that a beneficiary has predeceased the deceased. This is commonly known as a Benjamin order, following the principles laid down in *Re Benjamin* [1902] 1 Ch 723.

Limitations

Section 15(1) of the Limitation Act 1980 does not operate to time bar a claim for the recovery of an interest of an estate of a deceased person (*Earnshaw v Hartley* (1999) *The Times*, 29 April), nor is a beneficiary in possession able to sustain a claim for adverse possession against other beneficiaries who are absolutely entitled (s 9 of the Limitation Act 1980; *James v Williams* (1999) *The Times*, 13 April).

6.3 Payments of debts, etc

In both solvent and insolvent estates, the assets should be applied in priority for the funeral, testamentary and administration expenses, debts and other liabilities. The statutory order for the application of assets is given in s 34 of and Sched 1 to the Act. The practitioner should:

- ensure that debts be paid with due diligence;
- obtain a formal discharge or receipts for all payments made;
- obtain clearance for tax liability by submitting Form IHT30 to the Capital Taxes Office. In 'excepted estates' cases, automatic discharge is given 35 days after the grant is made, provided that it is not limited

to part of the estate and that an account has not been called for within that time;
- confirm that the Department of Social Services has no claim against the estate for overpayment or repayment of benefits. Liability for this may lie solely with the personal representative (*Secretary of State for Social Services v Solly* [1974] 3 All ER 922);
- ascertain whether any application has been made or is likely to be made under the Inheritance (Provision for Family and Dependants) Act 1975. Such application must be made within six months from the date of the grant, otherwise leave of the court is necessary (s 4 and see *Re Salmon* [1981] Ch 167);
- complete any outstanding contracts. The personal representative has a duty to perform contracts which the deceased had entered into and not completed before his death (*Youngmin v Heath* [1974] 1 All ER 461);
- consider whether any contingency fund should be set up to meet known liabilities which cannot be ascertained for the time being (for example, tax, claims under the Inheritance Act, etc) having due regard for any beneficiaries who may be prejudiced by such a fund.

6.4 Registration and distribution

6.4.1 Land

The practitioner should check the position as regards beneficial ownership of the land. A personal representative may apply for the registration of freehold and leasehold land (ss 4 and 8 of the Land Registration Act 1925). A representative who is registered as proprietor would seem to be in the same legal position as in the case of unregistered land (ss 43 and 44 of the Act). He transfers land to a beneficiary by making an assent in the prescribed form. The assent must be in writing, must name the person in whose favour it is made and be signed by the representative (s 36(4) of the Act). A representative who is entitled either as a trustee or beneficially may make an assent in his own favour (see 6.6 and Form 7.24).

However, it is not mandatory for a representative entitled as a trustee to be registered as a proprietor. The delivery to the Land Registry of an assent, transfer or appropriation together with the grant is sufficient for the registrar to register the new proprietor.

6.4.2 Stocks and shares

These may be transferred under Sched 1 to the Stock Transfer Act 1963, by application to the registrar of the company. Enclose the original stock or share certificate and an office copy of the grant.

6.4.3 Bank accounts, etc

These are transferred by written instructions to the bank accompanied by grant or an office copy of it.

6.4.4 National Savings certificates

The certificates may be withdrawn or transferred after registration of the grant.

6.4.5 Chattels

These may be transferred by manual delivery or assent. The assent need not be in writing, but it is highly desirable.

6.4.6 Legacies

These may be by cheque drawn on the executor or estate account.

Personal representatives may satisfy legacies by appropriating cash and assets of known value. They may not appropriate to themselves assets of an unknown or uncertain value without leave of the court or the consent of the other beneficiaries. To do so would be a breach of the self-dealing rule (*Kane v Radley-Kane* [1998] 3 All ER 753).

Obtain a receipt for moneys paid or chattels delivered to beneficiaries (see Forms 7.25 and 7.26).

6.5 Variations and disclaimers

The practitioner should consider whether dispositions are capable of being disclaimed or varied and advise accordingly, since if it is for the benefit of the deceased's dependants, this may effect a sizeable saving in Inheritance Tax payable.

The dispositions of the estate (testate or intestate) may be disclaimed or varied by the beneficiaries without incurring a charge for tax (s 142 of the Inheritance Tax Act 1984). The disclaimer or variation must:

- be made within two years of the deceased's death;
- be in writing and executed by all the persons whose benefit is affected by the instrument;
- identify the disposition (the will) and clearly identify the particular property being redirected;
- be supported by a written election (variations only). The election should be worded to confirm that s 142 of the Inheritance Act 1984 applies and it is made by all the persons executing the variation or by the personal representatives themselves if further tax is payable in connection with the death. The election may be incorporated in the instrument of variation, but if it is not, it must be made within six months of the date of the variation.

The effect of a disclaimer or variation is respectively to treat the benefit as if it had been conferred or it had been made by the deceased. It is not a transfer of value (s 17) and a tax liability may apply (see 7.23 for a form of assignment/variation and disclaimer).

For a detailed discussion on this subject see White, *Post-Death Rearrangements: Practice and Precedents*, 4th edn, 1992, London: Longman.

Where an order is made under the Inheritance (Provision for Family and Dependants) Act 1975, any property affected is treated as though it devolved on the death of the deceased (s 19).

6.6 Trust arrangements

Upon termination of the duties concerned with paying debts and distributing the non-trust estate, the personal representatives may have to act further as trustees. This role may arise under the terms of the will or according to law, as when property is held for the use and benefit of a minor, or a life interest arises.

The legal estate contained in trust property must be transferred to the trustee in accordance with s 36(4) of the Act. A personal representative who is also a trustee may make a written assent in his own favour (*Re King's Will Trusts* [1964] Ch 542).

6.7 Estate accounts and practitioner's costs

6.7.1 Accounts

The personal representative must keep an up to date and clear account of the estate. He must not mix the estate account with his own accounts. The account (see Form 7.19) should itemise all the capital assets followed by the debts and liabilities including the funeral account, inheritance and income tax liability, probate fees and professional charges (including the practitioner's) of acting in the estate. Added to the balance will be all the income and interest payable to the estate since death, and this is followed by an account of the distribution of legacies and the residuary estate itself including any interim payments.

The following matters should be clearly defined in the account:
- tax liability (including the distinction between income and capital gains/inheritance) during administration;
- distinction between capital and income receipts;
- any expenditure out of income payable to the personal representative; and
- the balance due for distribution.

6.7.2 Costs

The practitioner's bill of costs for work done must be presented before his charges are disbursed (see Form 7.20). There is no fixed scale of cost. These will reflect rates agreed before work was undertaken (s 57 of the Solicitors Act 1974) or calculated in accordance with the Solicitors (Non-Contentious Business) Remuneration Order 1994 SI 1994/216. The costs must be fair and reasonable taking particular account of:
- the complexity of the matter or the difficulty or novelty of the questions raised;
- the skill, labour, specialised knowledge and responsibility involved;
- the time spent on the business;
- the number and importance of documents (however brief) prepared, or perused without regard to length;
- the place where and the circumstances in which the business or any part of it is transacted;
- the amount or value of any money or property involved;
- whether any land involved is registered land;

- the importance of the matter to the client; and
- the approval (express or implied) of the person entitled or the express approval of the testator to:
  (a) the practitioner undertaking all or any part of the work giving rise to the costs; or
  (b) the amount of the costs.

These headings do not allow costs for work done to be duplicated or overlapped. They should be applied cumulatively to arrive at the sum charged.

If costs are agreed as a percentage of the value of the estate (appropriate if the estate is large), the percentage will reduce as the value of the estate increases (*Maltby v DJ Freeman* [1978] 2 All ER 913).

The practitioner must deliver his bill to his client and the residuary beneficiary. In the event of disagreement as to profit costs not exceeding £50,000, the client or beneficiary may require a solicitor practitioner to obtain a remuneration certificate from the Council of the Law Society. However, the client should first pay the disbursements, value added tax and 50% of the profit costs. This requirement may be waived by the solicitor or the Law Society in writing. Care must be taken to comply with the prescribed limits mentioned in Arts 7, 8 and 11 of the Order.

Alternatively, proceedings for assessment under ss 70–72 of the Solicitors Act 1974 may be begun in the Supreme Court Taxing Office. The solicitor will have to satisfy the court that his costs are fair and reasonable.

Section 27 of the Administration of Estates Act 1925 affords an executor protection for payments he makes out of the estate. However, it does not protect a solicitor recipient who, as executor, transfers sums from the estate in respect of the professional fees of his firm and himself if the will is subsequently declared invalid (*Gray v Richard Butler* (1996) *The Times*, 23 July).

A transfer of money from the estate to a solicitor's account with the knowledge of the trustees constitutes payment of the solicitor's bill and it is subject to the 12 month time limit in which a beneficiary could challenge the bill under s 70(4) of the Solicitors Act 1974.

7 Forms

7.1 Affidavit of due execution

See 8.1 for defects and particular difficulties which necessitate this affidavit.

IN THE HIGH COURT OF JUSTICE
FAMILY DIVISION
The [Principal Registry/District Probate Registry at   ]

In the estate of   deceased

I, [full name]   of [address]   , [occupation]   , make oath and say that

I am one of the attesting witnesses to the last Will and Testament of   , deceased, the said Will now being produced to me marked 'A'; the deceased executed the Will on the   day of   20   by signing his name at the foot or the end of it as it now appears [or state other position],

or

by acknowledging his signature by referring to it and pointing to it at the foot or the end of the Will as it now appears [or state other position],

or

by making his mark at the foot or at the end of it as it now appears [or state other position],

meaning and intending the same to be his final signature of the Will in the presence of [name of other witness], both of us being present at the same time;

we then signed the will in the presence of the deceased

[evidence of knowledge of contents]

and referring to his (feeble/imperfect/incomplete) signature/mark made in execution of the Will, previously to its execution the Will was read over to him by [name] or he read the will in our presence
and he seemed perfectly to understand it and have full knowledge and understanding of its contents.

[Evidence of alterations in the Will – see 8.2.]

and referring to the (deletions/additions/alterations) in the Will namely [describe the alterations] I confirm that they were made before execution of the will and the Will is now in all respects the same as it was when executed

or

they were not present in the will at execution and were made subsequently

or

I am unable to say/recollect whether they were made before the execution of the will

Sworn by the deponent

at

this   day of   20

Before me

A Commissioner for Oaths

7.2 Affidavit of handwriting

See 8.1.1 – this affidavit is required when evidence of execution of a will is not available but, coupled with this affidavit, it is possible to draw a presumption of due execution from surrounding circumstances.

IN THE HIGH COURT OF JUSTICE

FAMILY DIVISION

The [Principal Registry/]	District Probate Registry at
In the estate of	**deceased**
I [name] of [address],	[occupation]

make oath and say that

I have carefully perused and examined the paper writing purporting to be and to contain the last Will and Testament of AB of [address], deceased;

the Will dated the   day of   200   is now produced to me marked 'A';

I knew and was well acquainted with the deceased for   years preceding his death and frequently saw him write and sign his name and I am therefore well familiar with the manner and character of his handwriting;

I truly believe that the signature/name AB written at the foot [or other position] of the will to be the true and proper handwriting and signature of the deceased.

Sworn, etc [see 7.1 for jurat].

7.3 Affidavit of plight and condition

See 8.2 – this affidavit should account for the condition of the will when it was found after the death of the testator. It will deal with pin holes, punch holes, tears, burn marks, paperclip indentations.

IN THE HIGH COURT OF JUSTICE

FAMILY DIVISION

The [Principal Registry/District Probate Registry at   ]

In the estate of   deceased

I   [name] of   [address],   [occupation] make oath and say that

I am the sole executor named in the last Will and Testament of AB, deceased, the Will dated the   day of   200 now produced to me marked 'A'; and referring to the [condition of the Will, eg, torn edge, pinholes, punch holes, paperclip indentation etc.]

[confirm where the will was found after the death of the testator; account for its condition, for example, other papers attached to it by means of staple pin, paperclip which has since been removed; it was found in a punch file, it was found in an envelope, etc];

save as stated above the will is now in all respects in the same plight and condition as when found after the death of the testator.

Sworn, etc [see 7.1 for jurat].

7.4 Affidavit of search for a will

See 8.2 – this affidavit is required if the will is undated and no evidence is available to confirm the date; similarly if the will contains obliteration or alterations or the appearance of having had other papers attached to it.

IN THE HIGH COURT OF JUSTICE

FAMILY DIVISION

The [Principal/District Probate Registry at   ]

In the estate of   deceased

I   [name]   of [address]   , [occupation]

make oath and say that

I am the sole executor named in the last Will and Testament of AB, deceased, the Will now being produced to me marked 'A';

the will is not dated;

to the best of my information, knowledge and belief both the witnesses whose signatures and names appear in the Will are now dead and no one else was present when the deceased executed his Will;

I have been unable to obtain any information concerning the exact date of execution of the Will;

I have made inquiry of EG the deceased's solicitor and of his bank [exhibit any correspondence] and I have made a careful and diligent search of the deceased's possessions including places where he kept his important papers in search of any other will or testamentary papers but I have not discovered any and I know of no other person who may have kept papers for the deceased and I truly believe that the deceased died without having left any will other than the Will marked 'A'.

Sworn, etc [see 7.1 for jurat].

7.5 Affidavit in support of a privileged will

See 8.6.

IN THE HIGH COURT OF JUSTICE
FAMILY DIVISION
The [Principal Registry/District Probate Registry at   ]
In the estate of   deceased

I   [name] of   [address],   [occupation] make oath and say that

I am the sole executor named in the last Will and Testament of AB,

deceased who died on the   day of   200 , aged   years domiciled in England and Wales;

the Will dated the   day of   200 is now produced to me marked 'A';

at the date of the Will the deceased was a corporal in the 1st Battalion, the Parachute Regiment in actual military service and was taking part in military operations against rebel forces in Sierra Leone.

or

at the date of the will the deceased was a seaman at sea employed as First Officer on the motor vessel Chrysanthemum.

Sworn, etc [see 7.1 for jurat].

7.6 Affidavit of identity

See 3.12.

IN THE HIGH COURT OF JUSTICE
FAMILY DIVISION
The [Principal Registry/District Probate Registry at   ]
In the estate of Mary Elizabeth Lister   deceased

I, Catherine Elizabeth Barrel, of 6, Lynton Street, Oxford make oath and say that

Mary Elizabeth Lister deceased, died on the 10th day of September 2000 having made and duly executed her last Will and Testament dated the 1st day of December 1998 and in it she appointed Lisa Barrel of 6, Lynton Street, Oxford her sole executrix;

at the date of the will there was no one called Lisa Barrel residing at 6, Lynton Street, Oxford;

I was living at that address at the date of the Will;

I am commonly known now and since childhood as Lisa Barrel and the deceased referred to me as such; I was a godchild of the deceased and she informed me that she had appointed me her sole executrix;

I am unaware of any person other than myself called Lisa Barrel who was known to the deceased.

Sworn, etc [see 7.1 for jurat].

7.7 Affidavit in support of application for order to be appointed to obtain administration on behalf of a minor (r 32(2))

See 3.9.3.

IN THE HIGH COURT OF JUSTICE
FAMILY DIVISION

The [Principal Registry/District Probate Registry at   ]

In the estate of   AB   deceased

We CD of   [address and occupation] and EF of   [address and occupation]

jointly and severally make oath and say that

AB   of   , deceased died on the day of   200 , intestate, a widow aged [   ] years domiciled in England and Wales leaving SN her son and only person entitled to her estate who is now a minor aged [   ] years;

no one has parental responsibility for the minor and no one has been appointed his guardian in accordance with the Children Act 1989;

[if some person has parental responsibility for the minor or a guardian has been appointed and is entitled to take a grant give details here as to why the applicants wish to pass over this person];

the minor is not a ward of court nor the subject of proceedings which may affect his care and welfare and such proceedings are not currently contemplated;

the minor is not under the care or supervision of a local authority;

[supply details as to where the minor is residing, the arrangements of his day to day care and control since the death of the deceased and whether these arrangements will continue];

[give details of the applicants' connection or relationship with the minor specifying kinship, persons who have day to day control of the minor and any other facts in support of the application];

the gross value of the estate is £   and the net value is £   ;

in the circumstances we hereby apply for an order under r 32(2) of the Non-Contentious Probate Rules 1987 that letters of administration of the estate of the deceased be granted to us for the use and benefit of SN for his use and benefit until he attains the age of 18 years and until further representation be granted.

Sworn, etc [see form 7.1 for jurat].

7.8 Renunciation of probate (r 37)

See 1.5.

IN THE HIGH COURT OF JUSTICE

FAMILY DIVISION

The [Principal Registry/District Probate Registry at   ]

In the estate of   AB   deceased

Whereas   of   ,
deceased died on the   day of   200   , having made and duly executed his last Will and Testament dated the day of   200   and in the said will appointed   CD   the sole executor

Now I the said   CD   do hereby declare that I have not intermeddled in the estate of the deceased and will not hereafter intermeddle in it with intent to defraud creditors and I hereby renounce all my right and title to probate and execution of the said Will.★

Signed by the said CD as a deed

this   day of   200

in the presence of

[Signature and name of witness]

---

*   If the renunciant is appointed in any other capacity, eg, residuary legatee and devisee in trust, he should also renounce in that capacity (r 37(1)) by adding the following to this paragraph 'and to letters of administration with will annexed of the estate of the deceased'.

7.9   Renunciation of administration with will (r 37)

IN THE HIGH COURT OF JUSTICE
FAMILY DIVISION

The [Principal Registry/District Probate Registry at   ]

In the estate of   **AB**   **decease**

Whereas   AB   of   ,
deceased died on the   day of   200   , having
made and execute his last Will and Testament dated the   day of
200   and in the said appointed

CD the sole executor, who predeceased the deceased, and EF his wife as residuary legatee and devisee

Now I the said EF do hereby renounce all my right and title to letters of administration with the Will annexed of the estate of the said deceased.

Signed by the said EF as a deed

this   day of   200

in the presence of

[Signature and name of witness]

7.10 Renunciation of administration (r 37)

IN THE HIGH COURT OF JUSTICE

FAMILY DIVISION

The [Principal Registry/District Probate Registry at   ]

In the estate of   **AB**   deceased

Whereas AB, deceased died on the   day of   200   intestate leaving EF   his lawful widow and relict and only person now entitled to his estate

Now I the said EF do hereby renounce all my right and title to letters of administration of the estate of the said deceased.

Signed by the said EF as a deed

this   day of   200

in the presence of

[Signature and name of witness]

7.11 Renunciation of probate by two partners of a firm (r 37(2)(a))

This type of renunciation is made with the authority of the other members of a partnership; the rule requires that the renunciation should mention the authority and it is sufficient for the renouncing partners to confirm this merely by mentioning the authority.

IN THE HIGH COURT OF JUSTICE

FAMILY DIVISION

The [Principal Registry/District Probate Registry at   ]

In the estate of   **AB**   deceased

Whereas   AB of   , deceased died on the   day of   200 , having made and duly executed his last Will and Testament dated the   day of 200 and in the said Will appointed the partners at the date of his death in the firm of CD as his executors

The partners in the firm of CD at the date of the deceased's death were EF, GH, JK and LM

Now we the said EF and LM of [address] with the authority of the other said partners do hereby declare that neither we nor the other executors have intermeddled in the estate and we will not hereafter intermeddle therein with intent to defraud creditors and we do hereby renounce our right and title to probate and execution of the said Will.*

Signed by the said EF as a deed

this   day of   200

in the presence of

[Signature and name of witness]

Signed by the said LM, etc.

---

* If the partner executors are appointed in any other capacity, eg, residuary legatees and devisees in trust the renunciants should also renounce in that capacity (r 37(1)) by adding the following to this paragraph 'and to letters of administration with will annexed of the estate of the deceased'.

7.12 Retraction of renunciation (r 37(3))

Application for an order to retract a renunciation should be made to the registry where the original retraction is filed or to a district judge in the Principal Registry (r 37(4)); leave is given only in exceptional circumstances if a grant has already been made to a person with a lower title.

IN THE HIGH COURT OF JUSTICE
FAMILY DIVISION
The [Principal Registry/District Probate Registry at   ]

In the estate of   **AB**   **deceased**

AB of   , deceased died on the
day of 200   having made and duly executed his last will dated the
day of 200   and by it he appointed CD and myself EF his executors and residuary legatees and devisees in trust;

CD and I renounced probate and execution of the will and letters of administration (with will) of the estate of the deceased on the day of 200 ;

on the day of 200 letters of administration (with will) of the estate were granted to GH the residuary legatee and devisee named in the will who has since become mentally incapable;

by an order of Mr Registrar [   ] of this Division dated the   day of 200 I was given leave to retract my renunciation.

Now I EF do retract my renunciation of probate and execution of the will and letters of administration (with will) of the estate of AB deceased.

Signed by EF as a deed

this   day of   2000

in the presence of

[name and address of witness]

7.13 Caveat

See 5.1 and following pages.

IN THE HIGH COURT OF JUSTICE
FAMILY DIVISION
The [Principal Registry/District Probate Registry at   ]

In the estate of   deceased

Let no grant be sealed in the estate of [full name including alias names and if different the name given in the death certificate] deceased, who was born on the day of   19 /20 and who died on the day of   19 /20 without notice to

[name of person by whom or on whose behalf the caveat is entered]

Dated the   day of   20

[Signed by practitioner or caveator if acting in person

whose address for service is

Solicitor/probate practitioner for the said [caveator] or

Caveator in person

7.14 Warning to caveator (r 44(5))

See 5.5; a warning to a caveator must be filed in the Probate Registry in Leeds.

IN THE HIGH COURT OF JUSTICE
FAMILY DIVISION
The District Probate Registry at Leeds

In the estate of   **deceased**

To [caveator's name] of
a party who has entered a caveat in the estate of   deceased

You have eight days (starting with the day on which this warning was served on you):

(i) to enter an appearance either in person or by your solicitor or probate practitioner, at the District Probate Registry Leeds whose address is 3rd Floor, Coronet House, Queen Street, Leeds LS1 2BA or DX 26451 Leeds (Park Square), setting out what interest you have in the estate of the above named   of deceased contrary to that of the person at whose instance this warning is issued; or

(ii) if you have no contrary interest but to show cause against the sealing of the grant to such party, to issue and serve a summons for directions by a district judge of the Principal Registry or a registrar of a district probate registry.

If you fail to do either of these, the court may proceed to issue a grant of probate or administration in the said estate notwithstanding your caveat

Dated the   day of   200

Issued at the instance of [name and address for service of documents of person warning either through a solicitor, probate practitioner or in person – include also details of interest of person warning in the estate of the deceased including date of any will under which an interest arises]

Registrar

7.15 Appearance to warning or citation (rr 44(10), 47(4) and 48(2)(b))

See 5.5; an appearance to the warning of a caveat must be filed in the Probate Registry in Leeds.

IN THE HIGH COURT OF JUSTICE
FAMILY DIVISION
The District Probate Registry at Leeds [*if appearance is to a caveat*]

The Principal Registry/District Probate Registry [*if appearance is to a citation*]

Caveat No   dated the   day of
         200   or

Citation dated the   day of   200

In the estate of   deceased,

of

Full name and address of person warning or citor [including his interest as disclosed in the notice of warning or citation]

Full name and address of caveator or person cited [including his interest stating the date of any will under which an interest arises]

Enter an appearance for the above-named caveator [person cited] in this matter.

Dated the   day of   200

signed

whose address for service is

Solicitor/probate practitioner/in person

7.16 Standing search (r 43)

See 5.9; all alternative names of the deceased should be included in this form.

IN THE HIGH COURT OF JUSTICE
FAMILY DIVISION
The [Principal Registry/District Probate Registry at   ]

In the estate of   deceased

I/We apply for the entry of a standing search so that there shall be sent to me/us an office copy of every grant of representation in England and Wales in the estate of:

Full name of deceased

Full address

alternative or alias names

Date of death

Date of birth

which either has issued not more than twelve months before the entry of this application or issues within six months thereafter

Signed

Name in block letters

Full address

Reference No (if any)

7.17 Summons

See 5.8.

**IN THE HIGH COURT OF JUSTICE
FAMILY DIVISION
The [Principal Registry/District Probate Registry at   ]**

In the estate of   **deceased**

Between   CD
Applicant/Caveator

and   EF
Respondent

Let the parties attend before the District Registrar at the District Probate Registry at [address] or

[one of the judges of this Division in chambers at the Royal Courts of Justice, Strand, London WC2] or

[one of the district judges at the Principal Registry of the Family Division, First Avenue House, 42–49 High Holborn, London WC1V 6NP]

on   day the [date] day of [month] 20   at   o'clock

on the hearing of an application on the part of the Applicant for an order for [directions or order sought] or

to show cause why Caveat No   entered on the   day of   200 should not be discontinued and why probate of the will/letters of administration with the will dated the   day of   200   / letters of administration of AB, deceased should not be granted to CD the [title], if entitled and on application for a grant by the said CD the caveat do cease to have effect

This summons was taken out by   (solicitors)

of [address] for the Applicant

To EF [care of solicitors if instructed]

7.18 Nomination of second administrator (r 32(3))

See 3.9.3.

IN THE HIGH COURT OF JUSTICE
FAMILY DIVISION
The [Principal Registry/District Probate Registry at   ]

In the estate of   AB   deceased

AB of   , deceased died on the   day of   200 intestate domiciled in England and Wales leaving CD his lawful widow and EF his daughter together the only persons entitled to his estate;

EF is now a minor of   years of age;

I, CD, am the mother of EF and the only person with parental responsibility for her who is competent and willing to take a grant;

Now I, CD hereby nominate GH to act as my co-administrator in the estate of AB, deceased and confirm that he is a fit and proper person to act in that capacity.

Dated the day of   200

Signed by CD

in the presence of

[Name and address of witness]

7.19 Account

See 6.7.1.

In the estate of   **deceased**

late of

Date of death

Assets   £
HSBC (current account)
Barclays Bank (deposit account)
Nationwide Building Society
Treasury 8% Stock
Shares (as per schedule)
Life assurance:
    Equity and Law
    Commercial Union
    Legal and General
Household and personal effects
Cash   _____

                                  Total   _____

Less debts
Cook's Funeral Services
Income Tax/Inheritance Tax
Solicitor's fees
VAT
Disbursements: [itemise]
Other debts [eg, telephone, gas,
    electricity, etc]   _____

                                  Total   _____

                    Balance brought forward _____

Add income
Barclays Bank (net)
Nationwide Building Society (net)
Legal and General (gross)
Share dividend [itemise] (net)
Sale of household goods

    Final account for distribution   _____

7.20 Bill of costs

See 6.7.2.

Grant of representation:

Probate dated the   day of   200

In the estate of   **deceased**

Professional charges	£
VAT	£
Disbursements	£
	————
Total	£ ————

To professional charges attending you and taking your instructions to extract probate of the Will and last Testament of the deceased who died on the   day of   200

Conferring and discussing as to the deceased's estate, debts liabilities, funeral expenses and lifetime gifts.

Obtaining valuations of the deceased's house, securities, chattels, etc.

Confirming and verifying the deceased title to his house.

Preparing the Inland Revenue account to include all the deceased's real and personal property, debts, liabilities, funeral expenses and schedules as required.

Attending the Capital Taxes Office and paying the Inheritance Tax.

Preparing the executor's oath and advising as to swearing it.

Sending papers to the probate registry and paying the court fee.

Writing to various asset holders and producing the grant or office copies for registration.

Obtaining certificate of discharge from the Inland Revenue.

Preparing estate accounts and arrangements for distribution in accordance with the will of the deceased.

Attendance on and correspondence to you and general care and attention throughout.

Disbursements: £

Swearing fees

Court fees

Valuation fees

Registration fees

7.21 Section 27 notice

See 6.2.

In the estate of Matthew Kelly deceased

Notice is hereby given that any person having a claim against or an interest in the estate of Matthew Kelly late of 10 Lynton Road, Kettering, Northants KT1 2LM who died on the 30th day of August 2000 is required to send in writing his claim or interest to the undersigned who are the solicitors for the executors of the will of Matthew Kelly. This must be done on or before the 1st day of November 2000.★ After this date the said executors will proceed to distribute the assets of the deceased among the persons entitled to them, having regard only to the claims and interest of which they have had notice.

Dated the 30th day of August 2000★

Stephenson & Co

of 10 New Street

Bedford

★ At least two calendar months' notice should be given.

7.22 Advertisement for inclusion in a s 27 notice in the *London Gazette*

See 6.2.

Surname of deceased

other names

Address of deceased

Description (of the deceased)

Name and address of persons to whom notice of the claim should be given

Names of executors or administrators

Date by which notice must be given (at least two calendar months and one day's notice must be allowed)

Signed

Address

Capacity [the particulars must be signed by a solicitor or accountant]

7.23 Deed of assignment/variation and disclaimer

See 6.5.

This deed of Assignment [Variation] [Disclaimer] is made this 10th day of September 2000

between EVELYN DIGBY (the Wife) and PHILIP DIGBY and BEVERLEY JOHNSTON (the Children)

Whereas

JONATHAN DIGBY (the Deceased) died on the 25th day of May 2000 intestate leaving the Wife and the Children the only persons entitled as statutory beneficiaries to his estate (the estate) on his intestacy

The Children have attained the age of 18 years

The Children wish to disclaim their entitlement to the estate in favour of the Wife

NOW THIS DEED IRREVOCABLY WITNESSES as follows

1. The Children each hereby assign all their right and title to the estate to the Wife

2. By such assignment the Children disclaim all their right and title to the estate

3. The Wife and Children certify that this instrument falls within Category L in the Schedule to the Stamp Duty (Exempt Instruments) Regulations 1987

[4. The Wife and Children elect that the provisions of s 142(1) of the Inheritance Act 1984 and s 62(6) of the Taxation of Chargeable Gains Act 1992 shall apply to the variations made by this Deed]

Signed as a Deed and delivered

by EVELYN DIGBY

in the presence of

[witness]

Signed as a Deed and delivered

by PHILLIP DIGBY

in the presence of

[witness]

Signed as a Deed and delivered

by BEVERLEY JOHNSTON

in the presence of

[witness]

7.24 Assent of freehold property

See 6.4.1.

WE   of

and   of

being the personal representatives of   deceased

late of

who died on the   day of   2000 and

probate of whose will was granted to us on the   day of   2000 out
of the District Probate Registry at   do assent to the
vesting in [full name]

of all and singular the property specified in the Schedule herein for an estate in fee simple subject to the matters set out in it.

As witness my hand this   day of   2000

SCHEDULE

ALL that property, namely [full description of the property].

7.25 Receipt for legacies

See 6.4.6.

IN THE ESTATE OF MATTHEW KELLY DECEASED

I Hannah Neighbour acknowledge receipt of the sum of five hundred pounds (£500) from Hugo Kelly in satisfaction of the legacy due to me under the Will of the late Matthew Kelly

(signed) H Neighbour

Dated the 30th day of September 2000

7.26 Receipt for a bequest

See 6.4.6.

IN THE ESTATE OF MATTHEW KELLY DECEASED

I   of

acknowledge that I have received the Rolex watch left to me by the will of the late Matthew Kelly

Signed

Dated

7.27 Inland Revenue Account

Inland Revenue Account for Inheritance Tax

Fill in this account for the estate of a person who died on or after 18 March 1986. You should read the related guidance note(s) before filling in any particular box(es). The notes follow the same numbering as this form, so section headings are shown by capital letters and the items in each section are on a dark background.

A Probate Registry, Commissary Court or Sheriff Court District

Name **A1** OXFORD DISTRICT PROBATE REGISTRY   Date of Grant

B About the person who has died

Title **B1** MR.   Surname **B2** MASTERS
First name(s) **B3** JOHN DAVID
Date of birth **B4** 25/02/1930   Date of death **B5** 30/09/2000
Marital status **B6** Married
Surviving relatives   Last known usual address **B7** 10 Bedrock Avenue, Banbury, Oxfordshire
Husband/Wife **B8** ✓
Brother(s)/Sister(s) **B9**
Parent(s) **B10**   Postcode OX10 1OT
Number of
Children **B11** 2   Nursing / Residential home **B13**
Grandchildren **B12** 3   Domicile **B14** England and Wales
Occupation **B15** Retired
National Insurance number **B16** MN 61 24 05 D
Income tax district **B17** P.D.2
Income tax reference or self assessment reference **B18** 941/101

C Solicitor or other person to contact

Name and address of firm or person dealing with the estate
C1 Petty and Harris, 10 Old Road, Oxford
Postcode OX1 3WZ
Telephone number **C4** 01865 246163
Fax number **C5** 01865 211102

DX number and town
C2 DX 1826 OXFORD 1
Contact name and reference
C3 Mrs. H. Petty — HP001

For CTO use

IHT 200

R2H4114CTO11/99

Supplementary pages

You must answer all of the questions in this section. You should read the notes starting at page 10 of form IHT 210 before answering the questions.

If you answer "Yes" to a question you will need to fill in the supplementary page shown. If you do not have all the supplementary pages you need you should telephone our Orderline on 0845 2341000

		No	Yes	Page
• The Will	Did the deceased leave a Will?		✓	D1
• Domicile outside the United Kingdom	Was the deceased domiciled outside the UK at the date of death?	✓		D2
• Gifts and other transfers of value	Did the deceased make any gift or any other transfer of value on or after 18 March 1986?		✓	D3
• Joint assets	Did the deceased hold any asset(s) in joint names with another person?		✓	D4
• Nominated assets	Did the deceased, at any time during their lifetime, give written instructions (usually called a "nomination") that any asset was to pass to a particular person on their death?	✓		D4
• Assets held in trust	Did the deceased have any right to any benefit from any assets held in trust or in a settlement at the date of death?		✓	D5
• Pensions	Did the deceased have provision for a pension, other than the State Pension, from employers, a personal pension policy or other provisions made for retirement?		✓	D6
• Stocks and shares	Did the deceased own any stocks or shares?		✓	D7
• Debts due to the estate	Did the deceased lend any money, either on mortgage or by personal loan, that had not been repaid by the date of death?	✓		D8
• Life insurance and annuities	Did the deceased pay any premiums on any life insurance policies or annuities which are payable to either the estate or to someone else or which continue after death?		✓	D9
• Household and personal goods	Did the deceased own any household goods or other personal possessions?		✓	
• Interest in another estate	Did the deceased have a right to a legacy or a share of an estate of someone who died before them, but which they had not received before they died?	✓		D11
• Land, buildings and interests in land	Did the deceased own any land or buildings in the UK?		✓	D12
• Agricultural relief	Are you deducting agricultural relief?	✓		D13
• Business interests	Did the deceased own all or part of a business or were they a partner in a business?	✓		D14
• Business relief	Are you deducting business relief?	✓		D14
• Foreign assets	Did the deceased own any assets outside the UK?	✓		D15
• Debts owed by the estate	Are you claiming a deduction against the estate for any money that the deceased had borrowed from relatives, close friends, or trustees, or other loans, overdrafts or guarantee debts?	✓		D16

E Domicile in Scotland

- Has any claim for legal rights been made or discharged? **No** ✓ Yes
- How many children are under 18 ☐ or 18 and over ☐

F Estate in the UK where tax may not be paid by instalments

- Quoted stocks, shares and investments *(box SS1, form D7)* — **F1** £109610.69
- UK Government and municipal securities *(box SS2, form D7)* — **F2** £
- Unquoted stocks, shares and investments — **F3** £
- Traded unquoted stocks and shares — **F4** £4986.15
- Dividends or interest — **F5** £680.72
- Premium Bonds — **F6** £
- National Savings investments *(show details on form D17)* — **F7** £
- Bank and building society accounts *(show details on form D17)* — **F8** £3525
- Cash — **F9** £285
- Debts due to the deceased and secured by mortgage *(box DD1, form D8)* — **F10** £
- Other debts due to the deceased *(box DD1, form D8)* — **F11** £
- Rents due to the deceased — **F12** £
- Accrued income — **F13** £
- Apportioned income — **F14** £
- Other income due to the deceased *(box IP4, form D9, box PA1 form D6)* — **F15** £
- Life insurance policies *(box IP3, form D9)* — **F16** £96575
- Private health schemes — **F17** £
- Income tax or capital gains tax repayment — **F18** £
- Household and personal goods *(sold, box HG1, form D10)* — **F19** £
- Household and personal goods *(unsold, box HG2, form D10)* — **F20** £10 200
- Interest in another estate *(box UE1, form D11)* — **F21** £
- Interest in expectancy (reversionary interest) — **F22** £
- Other personal assets in the UK *(show details on form D17)* — **F23** £20 000

Total assets *(sum of boxes F1 to F23)* — **F24** £245862.56

Liabilities, funeral expenses, exemptions and reliefs

- Liabilities

Name	Description of liability	
Mastercard	Credit card liability	£2500
Medicare Ltd.	Care assistants	350
British Gas	Outstanding bill	75
Southern Electric	" " "	58
NTL	Cable TV and telephone	45
West Oxon D.C.	Council Tax	90

Total liabilities F25 £3118

- Funeral expenses

Dents Funeral Services	2125
Refreshments	250
Headstone	950

Total of funeral expenses F26 £3325

Total liabilities and funeral expenses *(box F25 plus box F26)* F27 £6443

Net total of assets less liabilities *(box F24 less box F27)* F28 £239419.56

- Exemptions and reliefs

Spouse Exemption

Total exemptions and reliefs F29 £5419.56

Chargeable value of assets in the UK where tax may not be paid by instalments *(box F28 less box F29)* F30 £234000

G Estate in the UK where tax may be paid by instalments

Do you wish to pay the tax on these assets by instalments? **No** / **Yes**

- Deceased's residence — G1 £
- Other residential property — G2 £
- Farms — G3 £
- Business property — G4 £
- Timber and woodland — G5 £
- Other land and buildings — G6 £
- Farming business — G7.1 £ (Interest in a business) — G7.2 £ (Interest in a partnership) — G7 £
- Other business interests — G8.1 £ (Interest in a business) — G8.2 £ (Interest in a partnership) — G8 £
- Business assets — G9.1 £ (Farm trade assets) — G9.2 £ (Other business assets) — G9 £
- Quoted shares and securities, control holding only — G10 £
- Unquoted shares — G11.1 £ (Control holding) — G11.2 £ (Non-control holding) — G11 £
- Traded unquoted shares — G12.1 £ (Control holding) — G12.2 £4986.15 x (Non-control holding) — G12 £4986.15 x

Total assets (sum of boxes G1 to G12) — G13 £4986.15

Liabilities, exemptions and reliefs

- Name and address of mortgagee — G14 £
- Other liabilities

Total of other liabilities — G15 £

Net total of assets less liabilities (box G13 less boxes G14 and G15) — G16 £4986.15

- Exemptions and reliefs

  Spouse Exemption

Total exemptions and reliefs — G17 £4986.15

Chargeable value of assets in the UK where tax may be paid by instalments (box G16 less box G17) — G18 £0

H Summary of the chargeable estate

You should fill in form IHT(WS) so that you can copy the figures to this section and to section J.
If you are applying for a grant without the help of a solicitor or other agent and you do not wish to
work out the tax yourself, leave this section and section J blank. Go on to section K.

Assets where tax may not be paid by instalments

- Estate in the UK *(box WS1)* — H1 £234000
- Joint property *(box WS2)* — H2 £0
- Foreign property *(box WS3)* — H3 £
- Settled property on which the trustees would like to pay tax now *(box WS4)* — H4 £

Total of assets where tax may not be paid by instalments *(box WS5)* — H5 £234000

Assets where tax may be paid by instalments

- Estate in the UK *(box WS6)* — H6 £
- Joint property *(box WS7)* — H7 £
- Foreign property *(box WS8)* — H8 £
- Settled property on which the trustees would like to pay tax now *(box WS9)* — H9 £

Total of assets where tax may be paid by instalments *(box WS10)* — H10 £

Other property taken into account to calculate the total tax

- Settled property *(box WS11)* — H11 £
- Gift with reservation *(box WS12)* — H12 £

Chargeable estate *(box WS13)* — H13 £
Cumulative total of lifetime transfers *(box WS14)* — H14 £
Aggregate chargeable transfer *(box WS15)* — H15 £234000

J Calculating the tax liability

Calculating the total tax that is payable

- Aggregate chargeable transfer *(box WS16)* — J1 £234,000
- Tax threshold *(box WS17)* — J2 £234,000
- Value chargeable to tax *(box WS18)* — J3 £0

  Tax payable *(box WS19)* — J4 £0

- Tax (if any) payable on lifetime transfers *(box WS20)* — J5 £
- Relief for successive charges *(box WS21)* — J6 £

  Tax payable on total of assets liable to tax *(box WS22)* — J7 £

Calculating the tax payable on delivery of this account

- Tax which may not be paid by instalments *(box TX4)* — J8 £
- Double taxation relief *(box TX5)* — J9 £
- Interest to be added *(box TX7)* — J10 £

  Tax and interest being paid now which may not be paid by instalments *(box TX8)* — J11 £

- Tax which may be paid by instalments *(box TX12)* — J12 £
- Double taxation relief *(box TX13)* — J13 £
- Number of instalments being paid now J14 ___ / 10 *(box TX15)*
- Tax now payable *(box TX16)* — J15 £
- Interest on instalments to be added *(box TX17)* — J16 £
- Additional interest to be added *(box TX18)* — J17 £

Tax and interest being paid now which may be paid by instalments *(box TX19)* — J18 £

Total tax and interest being paid now on this account *(box TX20)* — J19 £0

K Authority for repayment of inheritance tax

In the event of any inheritance tax being overpaid the payable order for overpaid tax and interest in connection with this estate should be made out to

L Declaration

I/We wish to apply for a **L1** Grant of Probate

To the best of my/our knowledge and belief, the information I/we have given and the statements I/we have made in this account and in supplementary pages **L2** D1 D3 D4 D6 D7 D9 D10 D12 D17 D18 attached (together called "this account") are correct and complete.

I/We have made the fullest enquiries that are reasonably practicable in the circumstances to find out the open market value of all the items shown in this account. The value of items in box(es) **L3** are provisional estimates which are based on all the information available to me/us at this time. I/We will tell Capital Taxes Office the exact value(s) as soon as I/we know it and I/we will pay any additional tax and interest that may be due.

I/We understand that I/we may be liable to prosecution if I/we deliberately conceal any information that affects the liability to inheritance tax arising on the deceased's death, OR if I/we deliberately include information in this account which I/we know to be false.

I/We understand that I/we may have to pay financial penalties if this account is incorrect by reason of my/our fraud or negligence, OR if I/we fail to remedy anything in this account which is incorrect in any material respect within a reasonable time of it coming to my/our notice.

I/We understand that the issue of the grant does not mean that

- I/we have paid all the inheritance tax and interest that may be due on the estate, or
- the statements made and the values included in this account are accepted by Capital Taxes Office.

I/We understand that Capital Taxes Office

- will only look at this account in detail after the grant has been issued
- may need to ask further questions and discuss the value of items shown in this account
- may make further calculations of tax and interest payable to help the persons liable for the tax make provision to meet the tax liability.

I/We understand that where we have elected to pay tax by instalments that I/we may have to pay interest on any unpaid tax according to the law.

Each person delivering this account, whether as executor, intending administrator or otherwise must sign below to indicate that they have read and agreed the statements above.

Full name and address	Full name and address
HANNAH MASTERS 70 Palace View Woodstock Oxfordshire OX8 7SV	
Signature *H. Masters* Date 28.10.2000	Signature Date
Full name and address	Full name and address
Signature Date	Signature Date

The Will

Name: JOHN DAVID MASTERS

Date of death: 30 / 09 / 2000

Give details about the latest Will made by the deceased. If a Deed of Variation has been signed before applying for a grant, fill in the form to show the effect of the Will and the Deed together. You should read form D1(Notes) before filling in this form.

1 Is the address for the deceased as shown in the Will the same as the address on page 1 of form IHT200? No ☐ Yes ✓

If the answer is "No", say below what happened to the property shown in the Will.

2 Are all items referred to in the Will, for example, legacies referring to personal possessions, stocks and shares, loans or gifts made by the deceased, included in form IHT200? N/A ☐ No ☐ Yes ✓

If the answer is "No", say below why these items are not included.

3 Does the whole estate pass to beneficiaries who are chargeable to inheritance tax? No ✓ Yes ☐

If the answer is "No", deduct the exemption on form IHT200.

Gift to Spouse:
GLADYS MASTERS
10 Bedrock Avenue
Banbury
Oxfordshire OX10 10T
Born 27.01.1931
Domiciled in England + Wales

D1

Gifts and other transfers of value

Name: JOHN DAVID MASTERS

Date of death: 30 / 09 / 2000

You have said that the deceased had transferred assets during their lifetime. Answer the following questions and give the further details we ask for. You should read form D3(Notes) before filling in this form.

1 Did the deceased within seven years of their death

1a make any gift or transfer to, or for the benefit of, another person? **No** ☐ **Yes** ✓

1b create any trust or settlement? **No** ✓ **Yes** ☐

1c pay any premium on a life insurance policy for the benefit of someone else other than the deceased's spouse? *(see also form D9, question 5)* **No** ✓ **Yes** ☐

1d cease to have any right to benefit from any assets held in trust or in a settlement? **No** ✓ **Yes** ☐

If the answer to any part of question 1 is "Yes", fill in the details we ask for below

Date of gift	Name and relationship of recipient and description of assets	Value at date of gift	Amount and type of exemption claimed	Net value after exemptions
1.11.98	Patrick Masters, Son, Cash	£9000	£3000 (annual 97/98)	£6000
24.1.2000	Elizabeth Perkins, Daughter, Cash – marriage gift	£10000	5000 (marriage)	5000
24.12.99	Hannah Masters, Daughter, Cash	5000		
24.12.99	Barry Masters, Son, Cash	5000		
24.12.99	Ross Masters, Son, Cash	5000		
		15000	6000 (annual 1998/99 1999/2000)	9000
			Total LT1	£20 000

D3

Gifts with reservation

2 Did the deceased transfer any assets during their lifetime but

2a the person receiving the gift did not take full possession of it, or **No** ✓ **Yes**

2b the deceased continued to have some right to benefit from all or part of the asset? **No** ✓ **Yes**

If the answer to either part of question 2 is "Yes", fill in the details we ask for below.

Date of gift	Name and relationship of recipient and description of assets	Value at date of death	Amount and type of exemption claimed	Net value after exemptions

Total **LT2** £

Earlier transfers

3 Did the deceased make any *chargeable* transfers during the 7 years before the earliest date of the gifts shown at boxes LT1 and LT2 above? **No** ✓ **Yes**

If the answer to question 3 is "Yes", fill in the details below, but do not include the value in any of the tax calculations.

Date of gift	Name and relationship of recipient and description of assets	Value at date of gift	Amount and type of exemption claimed	Net value after exemptions

Inland Revenue Capital Taxes Office

Joint and nominated assets

Name	Date of death
JOHN DAVID MASTERS	30 / 09 / 2000

Give details of any assets that the deceased owned jointly with another person or people. If necessary use a separate form for each item. Give details of any property that the deceased had nominated during their lifetime. You should read form D4(Notes) before filling in this form.

1 Bank and building society accounts, stocks, shares, unit trusts, household effects etc

If the value of the deceased's share is **not** the **whole** value, say

- who the other joint owner(s) is or are — GLADYS MASTERS, Spouse
- when the joint ownership began — 1980
- how much each joint owner provided to obtain the item — 50%
- who received the income or interest, if there was any — each owner equally
- who received the benefit of any withdrawals from bank or building society accounts, if any were made — each owner equally
- whether the item passes to other joint owner(s) by survivorship or under the deceased's Will or intestacy.

Details of each item	Whole value	Deceased's share
HSBC High Interest Account No. 123456	12000	6000
Nationwide Cashbuilder A/C 98765432	20000	10000

- Liabilities

	Total of assets	JP1 £ 16 000
	Total of liabilities	JP2 £
	Net assets *(box JP1 less box JP2)*	JP3 £ 16 000

- Exemptions and reliefs

Spouse exemption	16 000
Total exemptions and reliefs	JP4 £ 16 000
Net total of joint assets *passing by survivorship* where tax may not be paid by instalments *(box JP3 less box JP4)*	JP5 £ 0

D4

Please turn over

2 Land, buildings, business assets, control shareholdings and unquoted shares

Do you wish to pay tax on these assets by instalments?   No ✓   Yes

If the value of the deceased's share is **not** the whole value, say

- who the other joint owner(s) is or are — GLADYS MASTERS   Spouse
- when the joint ownership began — 1980
- how much each joint owner provided to obtain the item — 50% of deposit and mortgage repayments
- who received the income, if there was any
- whether the item passes to other joint owner(s) by survivorship or under the deceased's Will or intestacy.

Details of each item	Whole value	Deceased's share
10 Bedrock Avenue Banbury Oxfordshire OX10 10T	250 000	125 000

Total of assets JP6 £ 125 000

- Liabilities

Breezeblock Building Society — mortgage 49 High Street, Banbury, Oxon, OX10 4DU	55 000

Total of liabilities JP7 £ 55 000

Net assets (box JP6 less box JP7) JP8 £ 70 000

- Exemptions and reliefs

Joint tenancy — passes by survivorship	70 000

Total exemptions and reliefs JP9 £ 70 000

Net total of joint assets *passing by survivorship* where tax may be paid by instalments (box JP8 less box JP9) JP10 £ 0

3 Nominated property

If the deceased nominated any assets to any person, describe the assets below and show their value.

Include the assets in the appropriate box in section F of form IHT200.

Inland Revenue Capital Taxes Office — Pensions

Name: JOHN DAVID MASTERS
Date of death: 30/09/2000

Answer the following questions and give the further details we ask for about the provision for pension(s) made by the deceased. You should read form D6(Notes) before filling in this form.

1. Did any payments made under a pension scheme or a personal pension policy continue after the deceased's death? **No ✓** Yes

If the answer is "Yes" give details below

Total **PA1** £

Include the figure from box PA1 in box F15, page 3, IHT 200.

2. Was a lump sum payable under a pension scheme or a personal pension policy as a result of the deceased's death? No **Yes ✓**

If the answer is "Yes" give details below

Local Government Superannuation Scheme lump sum payable to personal representative — 20 000

Total **PA2** £ 20 000

If the lump sum was payable as described in the notes, include the total from box PA2 in box F23, page 3, IHT 200.

3. Did the deceased, within 2 years of the death
- dispose of any of the benefits payable, or
- make any changes to the benefits to which they were entitled under a pension scheme or a personal pension policy?

No ✓ Yes

If the answer is "Yes" give details below

D6

Stocks and shares

Inland Revenue Capital Taxes Office

Name: JOHN DAVID MASTERS

Date of death: 30 / 09 / 2000

Give details about the stocks and shares included in the deceased's estate. You should read form D7(Notes) before filling in this form.

1 Quoted stocks, shares and investments *(see box 2 for government securities)*

Name of company and type of shares or stock, or full name of unit trust and type of units	Number of shares or units or amount of stock held	Market price at date of death	Total value at date of death	Dividend or interest due to date of death	For CTO use only
M+G Financial Services PLC PEP High Yield Corporate Bond Fund Income Unit	10720	52p	5574.40	28	
Scottish Widows Unit Trust Managers High Interest Fund Units	7495	109.51	7877.25	91.10	
Barclays Bank PLC	3541	1794	63525.54	244.10	
BG	1550	427	6618.50	98.50	
Thames Water	2150	1210	26015	120	
		Total(s) SS1	£109610.69	£581.70	

Copy the total from box SS1 to box F1, page 3, form IHT200.
Include the total of all dividends and interest in box F5, page 3.

D7

2 UK Government and municipal securities

Description of stock	Amount of stock £	Market price at date of death	Total value at date of death	Interest due to date of death	For CTO use only
		Total(s) SS2	£	£	

Copy the total from box SS2 to box F2, page 3, form IHT200.
Include the total of all dividends and interest in box F5, page 3.

3 Unquoted stocks, shares and investments

Name of company and type of share or stock	Number of shares	Price per share	Total value of shares	Dividend due to date of death	For CTO use only

Include the value of the shares in box F3, page 3 or box G11, page 5, form IHT200.
Include the total of all dividends in box F5, page3.

4 Traded unquoted stocks and shares

Name of company and type of share or stock	Number of shares	Price per share	Total value of shares	Dividend due to date of death	For CTO use only
Online Travel	2500	40.5p	1012.50	—	
Biofocus	885	449	3973.65	99	

Include the value of the shares in box F4, page 3 or box G12, page 5, form IHT200.
Include the total of all dividends in box F5, page 3.

Life insurance and annuities

Name: JOHN DAVID MASTERS
Date of death: 30 / 09 / 2000

Give details about the life insurance policies and annuities that the deceased paid premiums for. You should read form D9(Notes) before filling in this form.

1 Were any sums payable by insurance companies to the estate as a result of the deceased's death?   **No** ☐ **Yes** ✓

If the answer is "Yes" give details below

Scottish Widows Endowment	55125
Equitable Life	41 450

Total IP1 £96575

2 Was the deceased

2a a life assured under a joint life insurance policy which continues after death, or   **No** ✓ **Yes** ☐

2b entitled to benefit from a life insurance policy on the life of another person where the policy continues after death?   **No** ✓ **Yes** ☐

If the answer to either part of question 2 is "Yes" give details below

Total IP2 £

Total value for life insurance policies *(box IP1 plus box IP2)*   IP3 £96575
Copy the total from box IP3 to box F16, page 3, form IHT200.

D9

Please turn over

3 Did any payments made under a purchased life annuity continue after the deceased's death?   No ✓ Yes

If the answer is "Yes" give details below

Total IP4 £

Include the total from box IP4 in box F15, page 3, form IHT200.

4 Was a lump sum payable under a purchased life annuity as a result of the deceased's death?   No ✓ Yes

If the answer is "Yes" give details below

Total IP5 £

Include the total from box IP5 in box F23, page 3, form IHT200.

5 Did the deceased, within 7 years of their death, pay any premium on a life insurance policy for the benefit of someone else, other than the deceased's spouse?   No ✓ Yes

6 Did the deceased have some right to benefit from a life insurance policy taken out on another person's life and held in trust for the benefit of the deceased (and others)?   No ✓ Yes

If the answer to either question 5 or 6 is "Yes" you should read form D9(Notes) to find out what you should do.

Household and personal goods

Name: JOHN DAVID MASTERS

Date of death: 30 / 09 / 2000

Give details about the household goods or other personal property owned by the deceased. You should read form D10(Notes) before filling in this form.

1 If any household goods and other personal possessions have **already been sold**, fill in the gross sale proceeds below.

Gross proceeds of sale **HG1** £

Copy the value from box HG1 to box F19, page 3, form IHT200.

2 If you have obtained any valuation(s) of the household goods and other personal possessions that have not been sold, enter the total figure in the box below.

If no valuation has been obtained, give brief details of the items and their value.

Item	Value
2 Rolex watches : 2 × 1125	2150
Personal jewellery : gold rings (2)	250
Clothing (donated to Charity)	100
Ford Mondeo car (Reg.)	5000
Collection of walking sticks	500
Antiquarian books	700
Photographic equipment	1500

Total value of household and personal goods unsold **HG2** £10 200

Copy the value from box HG2 to box F20, page 3, form IHT200.

3 Are any of the unsold items going to be sold?   Unknown ☐ No ☐ Yes ✓

4 Say below how the value for the unsold items has been established. If you have given a low total value, or the value is "Nil", say why this is so.

Valuation attached

D10

Inland Revenue Capital Taxes Office

Land, buildings and interests in land

Name: JOHN DAVID MASTERS

Date of death: 30 / 09 / 2000

CTO reference:

Give the details we ask for about the land included in the deceased's estate. You should read form D12(Notes) before filling in this form.

1
Name and address of the person that the Valuation Office should contact

Reference

Telephone number

2

A Item No.	B Full address (including postcode) or description of property	C Tenure	D Lettings/leases	E Agricultural, timber or heritage element	F Open market value
	10 Bedrock Avenue, Banbury, Oxfordshire OX10 1OT. Matrimonial home held as joint tenancy with spouse. Deceased's share is £125 000.	freehold	—	—	250 000

Total(s) carried forward £ 250 000

D12

Please turn over

A Item No.	B Full address (including postcode) or description of property	C Tenure	D Lettings/leases	E Agricultural, timber or heritage element	F Open market value
			Total(s) brought forward	£	£
			Total(s)	£	£

3 Were any of the properties subject to any damage that may affect their value? No ✓ Yes ☐

If the answer is "Yes", fill in the box below using the same item number(s) that you have used in column A above.

Item No.	Details of damage

4 Have any of the properties been sold, or do you intend to sell any of them within 12 months? No ✓ Yes ☐

If the answer is "Yes", fill in table below using the same item number(s) that you have used in column A above.

Item No.	H Present position of sale	I Sale price	J Type of sale	K Price for fixtures, carpets and curtains	L Use sale price as value

Continuation sheet for additional information

Name: JOHN DAVID MASTERS

Date of death: 30 / 09 / 2000

Use this form as a continuation sheet or to give any additional information that we ask for. Show the box number on form IHT200 or the supplementary page number the information relates to. You should read form D17(Notes) before filling in this form.

Box or page number	Additional information	£
F8	HSBC Current Account	1200
	Nationwide Cashbuilder	2325
		3525
F23	See D6	

D17

Please turn over

Box or page number	Additional information	£

Probate summary

Fill in this page to give details of the estate that becomes the property of the personal representatives of the deceased. It is this property for which the grant of representation is to be made. You should read form D18(Notes) before filling in this form.

A Name and address

Petty and Harris
10 Old Road
Oxford
OX1 3WZ   DX1826

Probate registry
OXFORD

Date of grant (for probate registry use)

B About the person who has died

Title: Mr.   Surname: MASTERS
First name(s): JOHN DAVID

Date of death: 30 / 09 / 2000
Domicile: England and Wales

Last known usual address:
10 Bedrock Avenue
Banbury
Oxfordshire
Postcode OX10 10T

C Summary from IHT200
Add the value of any general power property on form D5 to boxes PS1-PS5

Gross assets, section F, box 24	PS1	£ 245862.56
Gross assets, section G, box 13	PS2	£ 4986.15
Gross value to be carried to Probate papers *(box PS1 plus box PS2)*	PS3	£ 250848.71
Liabilities, section F, box F27	PS4	£ 6443
Liabilities, section G, boxes G14 plus G15	PS5	£
Net value to be carried to Probate papers *(box PS3 less box PS4 less box PS5)*	PS6	£ 244405.71
Tax and interest paid on this account, section J, box J19	PS7	£ NIL

Signature of person or firm calculating the amount due: Han J Petty
Contact name and/or reference: HP001
Date: 28 / 10 / 2000

(For CTO use only)
CTO reference:
EDP:
Cashier's reference:
CTO Cashiers:

D18

Domicile outside the United Kingdom

Inland Revenue — Capital Taxes Office

Name: JOHN DAVID MASTERS

Date of death: 30 / 09 / 2000

You have said that the deceased was not domiciled in the United Kingdom. Answer the following questions and give the further details we ask for. You should read form D2(Notes) before filling in this form.

1 Write a brief history of the life of the deceased. If the deceased was female, and had married at any time on or before 1 January 1974, include a history of the life of the deceased's husband (or husbands) while she was married and up until 1 January 1974.

> The Deceased was born on 25.02.1930 in Thetford, Suffolk. He was educated at Thetford Grammar School and went on to University at Durham. He qualified as an engineer in 1952. Shortly afterwards he travelled to South Africa where he worked for Lonrho. He returned to the United Kingdom in 1960 where he joined Northamptonshire County Council's Engineering Department. He retired in 1990 and bought an apartment in the Algarve, Portugal. Together with his wife he set up his permanent abode in Portugal in 1991. He returned to England for brief holidays and family visits. In each year he stayed in the United Kingdom for only two weeks. He died in Portugal.

2 Was the deceased domiciled in the UK at any time during the 3 years up to the date of death? **No ✓** Yes

3 Was the deceased resident in the UK for income tax purposes during the 3 years up to the date of death? **No ✓** Yes

If the answer is "Yes" give details of any periods that the deceased was treated as resident in the UK during the last 20 years.

D2

Please turn over

4 Who will benefit from the deceased's estate under the law that applies in the country of domicile?

GLADYS MASTERS, Spouse.

5 Do you claim surviving spouse exemption?   No ☐   Yes ✓

If you have answered "No" go on to question 6 below. If you have answered "Yes", provide the details we ask for below.

5a Give brief details of the property the surviving spouse will receive following the death.

5b Was a community of property established in the foreign country?   No ✓   Yes ☐

If you have answered "No" go on to question 6. If you have answered "Yes" give full details of the rights each party to the marriage had over property.

5c Was any property under the community situated in the UK at the date of death?   No ☐   Yes ☐

If you have answered "Yes" give full details of the property.

5d Has the form IHT200 been completed on the basis of the community?   No ☐   Yes ☐

6 Did the deceased leave any assets of any description outside the UK?   No ☐   Yes ✓

If so, give their approximate value. £50 000

7 Do you expect the terms of a Double Taxation Convention or Agreement to apply to any or all of the foreign assets owned by the deceased?   No ☐   Yes ✓

8 Is any foreign tax to be paid on assets in the UK as a result of the deceased's death?   No ✓   Yes ☐

8 Answers to Common Problems

8.1 Matters that question due execution of a will

- No attestation clause.
- Defective attestation clause.
- Testator's signature not at the foot of the will.
- Testator's signature is below or between the witnesses' signatures.
- Testator's signature not apparent on the face of the will.
- Testator's feeble signature not accompanied by an attestation clause confirming reading over and knowledge of contents.
- Will not dated.

Rule 12 applies, as these matters raise questions about due execution of the will. Consider what evidence is available and whether it is necessary to prepare affidavit evidence. The registrar may allow the applicant to prove the will if no one is prejudiced by it, that is, the distribution of the estate would be the same if the deceased died intestate. Place these matters before the registrar either by attending at the registry or in writing. He may, depending on the circumstances of the case, dispense with evidence of execution from a witness, for example, if distribution under the will would be the same if the deceased had died intestate or the persons prejudiced by the will consent in writing. Where evidence is necessary, it should be given by one of the witnesses. If for good reason it is not convenient to prepare witness evidence – because they are deceased, infirm, not conveniently available, reluctant or not co-operative – obtain the registrar's direction for affidavit evidence by some other source such as a person who was present at execution or who drafted the will, etc.

The affidavit should confirm due execution and speak of the particular matters which require the evidence to be given (see Form 7.1), for example:

- the testator's signature was feeble because he was suffering from physical infirmity, but that the will was read over to him by a named person and he appeared to understand it perfectly. If the testator actually made any comment about his understanding of the will, this should be stated in the affidavit;
- that the testator wrote out his name, intending it to be his signature, at the beginning of the will (or in the margin) followed by the dispositions and that all the writing was made in one transaction (*Wood v Smith* [1991] 2 All ER 239).

8.1.1 No evidence of execution available

Obtain the directions of the registrar. He may accept any evidence which would satisfy a presumption that the will was duly executed. This may include evidence of the testator's handwriting, evidence of persons not present at execution who were aware of the circumstances surrounding the making of the will or were informed of this by the testator, entries in the testator's diary, etc.

As a last resort, the maxim *omnia (praesumuntur) rite esse acta* may allow a presumption of due execution to be made. The maxim allows the court to make a reasonable inference when:

- the testator's intention to do a formal act (make a will) is established; and
- the testator has carried out the act (his signature and those of the witnesses are written in the document; but
- the actual formality of carrying out the act can only be inferred (because the document has no attestation clause or the clause is defective or has some other defect);
- that it is more probable that what the testator intended to do (execute his will) was done as it ought to have been done (comply with s 9 of the Wills Act 1837) (*Harris v Knight* (1890) 15 PD 170).

8.2 What evidence is required if the will contains alterations, obliterations or interlineations which have not been formally authenticated by the testator and the witnesses or the will is not dated?

Rules 12 and 14 apply. An affidavit of execution should be obtained (Form 7.1). It should confirm the facts by making specific reference to the defect and the condition of the will at the time of execution. For example, it will confirm whether alterations were present in the will at the time of execution or the correct date of execution. In the absence of a date, or if the date is defective and the witness is unable to remember the date, he should narrow it down as closely as possible between two dates.

If the practitioner is unable to obtain the evidence of the witnesses, he should obtain affidavit evidence of plight and condition and of search for any other testamentary papers (Forms 7.3 and 7.4). This should confirm that the will was not altered by some person after the testator died or that the testator did not make alterations as a prelude to making another will.

If the evidence confirms that the will was altered after execution, or alterations cannot be accounted for, then unless they are of no practical importance, the registrar will direct that a fiat copy of the will be prepared for proof. A fiat copy reproduces the will in the form it existed before alterations were made.

An obliteration of a testator's signature by him or at his direction so that it cannot be read with a magnifying glass is a sufficient intention to revoke the whole will in the absence of any other explanation (*Re Adams* [1990] 2 All ER 97).

8.3 The original will has tears or burn marks, has pin holes or paperclip indentations

Refer the will to the registrar for directions as to evidence he requires to confirm validity. The nature of the tearing may create a presumption that the testator revoked his will by such tearing or burning (s 20 of the Wills Act 1837) and affidavit evidence to rebut this presumption is usually required. Evidence of plight and condition of the will when it was found after the testator's death may also be required, and this can be combined with the affidavit dealing with the burning or tearing.

Pin holes, paperclip indentations or an appearance of something previously attached to the will raise a suspicion that other testamentary documents may have been attached to the will. Again, an affidavit of plight and condition combined with evidence for search of other testamentary papers will usually be required.

8.4 The original will cannot be found; the applicant wishes to prove it as contained in a copy or a reconstruction

An application by affidavit for an order to prove the will as contained in a copy or reconstruction is required (r 54). Evidence should be filed to rebut the presumption that the will was revoked by the testator by destruction and with the intention to revoke it. Submit draft evidence for the registrar's perusal and comment.

Rebuttals may include confirmation that:
- the original will was not in the testator's possession, but it was in the safe keeping of his solicitor or bank and he could not have had the opportunity to destroy it;
- it was in existence after his death and cannot now be found;
- the testator's habit and custom were such (giving details) that he would not have revoked his will by destruction without notice to some person;
- the testator spoke of or discussed his will before and in the period leading up to his death.

The evidence should also confirm the authenticity of the copy will or reconstruction being produced for proof. The registrar may call for evidence of execution (Form 7.1) as well as an affidavit from the person who prepared the copy or reconstruction to verify its authenticity and contents.

The registrar's order will direct that the grant be limited until the original will or a (more) authentic copy be proved.

8.5 A sole executor who takes no benefit cannot be traced

A citation to take a grant may not be a practical procedure if the executor has not intermeddled. Place the facts before the registrar with a view to obtaining his direction to make an application under s 116 of the Supreme Court Act 1981 passing over the rights of the executor. This may be particularly appropriate where the distribution under the will is the same as for an intestacy. Submit a draft affidavit for the registrar's perusal and comment in the first instance.

8.6 Setting up a privileged will

An affidavit (Form 7.5) should be filed confirming that:

- the testator was domiciled in England and Wales or, if this is not the case, that the law of his domicile at the date of the will allowed him the right to make a privileged will (separate evidence of this law will also be required);
- the will is in his handwriting or, if not, it was made at his direction;
- affidavit evidence of the person who wrote the will is also necessary;
- at the date of execution, the testator was in actual military service (soldier) or was at sea (sailor or mariner).

An application for an order to prove a nuncupative will should be supported by an affidavit of facts and accompanied by the written and witnessed consents of the persons prejudiced.

8.7 The appointment of executor is ambiguous or appears to be void

This may arise where the wording of the appointment is of *one of the partners* or *a partner* of a firm or to *A or B* or similar. The appointment is potentially void for uncertainty if it does not indicate by words or expression which particular one of many persons the testator intended should act. Obtain the registrar's directions for the submission of evidence. The difficulty is usually one of interpretation and it may be resolved by evidence under s 21 of the Administration of Justice Act 1982. However, s 20 of this Act allows the court to rectify the will if the will does not reflect the testator's as a result of a clerical error in drafting or failure to understand the testator's instructions. The evidence should confirm the testator's instructions and intentions for an effective appointment of executor; if more than one person is mentioned, whether one is in substitution of the other and in what event the substitution takes effect. Sections 20 and 21 apply to cases where death occurred after 1 January 1983.

8.8 The person entitled in priority to a grant of representation is mentally incapable

Rule 35 applies. The intended applicant lodges a current medical certificate which confirms the mental incapacity of the person entitled (the patient) giving brief details. The medical practitioner should include also his opinion about the patient's recovery within three months from the date of the examination.

The applicant may be entitled to obtain a grant for the use and benefit of the patient if he is (in order of priority):
- the person authorised by the Court of Protection to apply for a grant on behalf of the patient;
- the lawful attorney of the patient acting under a registered power of attorney;
- the person entitled to the residuary estate – if there is no such lawful attorney or if the lawful attorney has renounced.

If the applicant does not qualify under the above headings, he may apply to the registrar for an order that he be appointed to obtain a grant for the use and benefit of the patient. He makes such application without notice by filing an affidavit in support. It is advisable in the first instance to set out the facts together with a draft affidavit for the registrar to comment on. At least two applicants are required to obtain representation if life or minority interests arise in the estate (s 114(2) of the Supreme Court Act 1981).

Unless the intended applicant is authorised to apply for the grant, notice of an application for a grant for the use and benefit of a patient must be given to the Court of Protection. That court will return a sealed acknowledgment of the notice to the practitioner and this must be filed with the oath to lead to the grant.

8.9 Remuneration to a professional executor

An executor who is entitled to charge for his services in the ordinary course of his business may do so if the will contains a charging clause. The charging clause is regarded as a legacy and it can be avoided or lost if the executor or his spouse witnessed the will. In this event, however, if the executor does not prove the will, but he is appointed at a later date as a trustee, he is entitled to charge profit costs for his services (*Re Royce's Will Trusts* [1959] 3 All ER 278, concerning a solicitor's right to charge).

9 Useful Addresses

Principal Registry of the Family Division
Probate Department
First Avenue House
42–49 High Holborn
London WC1V 6NP
DX 941 London/Chancery Lane
Tel 020 7947 7000
Fax 020 7947 6946

DISTRICT PROBATE REGISTRIES

Registry	**Sub-registry**
Birmingham	*Stoke on Trent*
The Priory Courts	Combined Court Centre
33 Bull Street	Bethesda Street
Birmingham	Hanley
B4 6DU	Stoke on Trent ST1 3BP
Tel 0121 681 3400	Tel 01782 854065
Fax 0121 236 2465	Fax 01782 274916
DX 701990 Birmingham 7	DX 20736 Hanley
Brighton	*Maidstone*
William Street	The Law Courts
Brighton	Barker Road
BN2 2LG	Maidstone ME18 8EW
Tel 01273 684071	Tel 01622 202048/7
Fax 01273 625845	Fax 01622 754384
DX 98073 Brighton 3	DX 130066 Maidstone 7

Bristol
Ground Floor, The Crescent Centre,
The Crescent Centre
Temple Back
Bristol BS1 6EP
Tel 0117 927 3915/926 4619
Fax 0117 925 3549
DX 94400 Bristol 5

Cardiff – Probate Registry of Wales
PO Box 474
2 Park Street
Cardiff CF10 1TB
Tel 029 20 376479
Fax 029 20 376266
DX 122782 Cardiff 13

Ipswich
Level 3, Haven House
17 Lower Brook Street
Ipswich
IP4 1DN
Tel 01473 253724/259261
Fax 01473 231951
DX 3279 Ipswich

Bodmin
Market Street
Bodmin
PL31 2JW
Tel 01208 72279
Fax 01208 269004
DX 81858 Bodmin

Exeter
Finance House
Barnfield Road
Exeter EX1 1QR
Tel 01392 274515
Fax 01392 493468
DX 8380 Exeter

Bangor
Council Offices
Fford Gwynedd
Bangor LL57 1DT
Tel 01248 362410
Fax 01248 364423
DX 23186 Bangor 2

Carmarthen
14 Kings Street
Carmarthen SA31 1BL
Tel 01267 236238
Fax 01267 229067
DX 51420 Carmarthen

Norwich
Combined Court Building
The Law Courts
Bishopsgate
Norwich NR3 1UR
Tel 01603 728267
Fax 01603 627469
DX 5202 Norwich

Peterborough
1st Floor, Crown Buildings
Rivergate
Peterborough PE1 1EJ
DX 112327 Peterborough 1

Leeds
3rd Floor, Coronet House
Queen Street
Leeds LS1 2BA
Tel 0113 243 1505
Fax 0113 247 1893
DX 26451 Leeds (Park Square)

Liverpool
Queen Elizabeth II Law Courts
Derby Square
Liverpool L2 1XA
Tel 0151 236 8264
Fax 0151 227 4634
DX 14246 Liverpool 1

Manchester
9th Floor, Astley House
23 Quay Street
Manchester M3 4AT
Tel 0161 834 4319
Fax 0161 832 2690
DX 14387 Manchester

Newcastle upon Tyne
2nd Floor, Plummer House
Croft Street
Newcastle upon Tyne NE1 6NP
Tel 0191 261 8383
Fax 0191 230 4868
DX 61081 Newcastle upon Tyne

Lincoln
360 High Street
Lincoln
LN5 7PS
Tel 01522 523648
Fax 01522 539903
DX 703233 Lincoln 6

Sheffield
PO Box 832
The Law Courts
50 West Bar
Sheffield S3 8YR
Tel 0114 281 2596
Fax 0114 281 2598
DX 26054 Sheffield 2

Chester
5th Floor, Hamilton House
Hamilton Place
Chester CH1 2DA
Tel 01244 345082
Fax 01244 346243
DX 22162 Northgate

Lancaster
Mitre House
Church Street
Lancaster LA1 1HE
Tel 01524 36625
Fax 01524 35561

Nottingham
Butt Dyke House
Park Row
Nottingham NG1 6GR
Tel 0115 941 4288
Fax 0115 950 3383
DX 10055 Nottingham

Carlisle
Courts of Justice
Earls Street
Carlisle CA1 1DJ
Tel 01228 521751
DX 63034

Oxford
Combined Court Building
St Aldates
Oxford OX1 1LY
Tel 01865 793050
Fax 01865 793090
DX 96454 Oxford

Winchester
4th Floor, Cromwell House
Andover Road
Winchester SO23 7EW
Tel 01962 853046/863771
Fax 01962 840796
DX 96900 Winchester 2

Middlesbrough
Teesside Combined Court
Russell Street
Middlesbrough TS1 2AE
Tel 01642 340001
DX 60536 Middlesbrough

York
Duncombe Place
York YO1 2EA
Tel 01904 671564
Fax 01904 624210
DX 61543

Gloucester
Combined Court Building
Kimbrose Way
Gloucester GL1 2DG
Tel 01452 522585
Fax 01452 421849
DX 7537 Gloucester

Leicester
5th Floor, Leicester House
Lee Circle
Leicester LE1 3RE
Tel 0116 253 8558
Fax 0116 261 9023
DX 13665 Leicester 4

OTHER ADDRESSES

Capital Taxes Office
Ferrers House
PO Box 38
Castle Meadow
Nottingham NG2 1BB
DX 701201 Nottingham 4
Tel 0115 974 2400 (Helpline)

Public Trust Office/Court of Protection
Stewart House
24 Kingsway
London WC2B 6JX
DX 141150 Kingsway
Tel 020 7664 7000

Treasury Solicitor (BV)
Queen Anne's Chamber
28 Broadway
London SW1H 9JS

or

DX 123240 St James's Park
Tel 020 7201 3115/6/7

10 Further Reading

Aldridge, T, *Powers of Attorney*, 9th edn, 2000, London: Sweet & Maxwell

Atkin's Court Forms, London: Butterworths, available on CD-ROM

Bark-Jones, R (ed), *Wills, Probate and Administration Service*, 1996, London: Butterworths looseleaf

Clark, J, *Theobald on Wills*, 16th edn, 2000, London: Sweet & Maxwell

D'Costa, R, *Holloway's Probate Handbook* 9th edn, 1993, London: Sweet & Maxwell

Heywood, N and Massey, A, *Court of Protection Practice*, 12th edn, 1991, London: Sweet & Maxwell

Tristram and Coote's Probate Practice, 28th edn, 1995, London: Butterworths (supplements – 1998 and 2000)

Sunnucks, JHG, *Executors, Administrators and Probate*, 18th edn, 1993, London: Sweet & Maxwell